Debts Hopeful and Desperate Financing the Plymouth Colony

By

Ruth A. McIntyre

Double9 BOOKS

Debts Hopeful and Desperate Financing the Plymouth Colony

by **Ruth A. McIntyre**

ISBN: 978-93-58716-57-3

Published by

DOUBLE 9 BOOKS
2/13-B, Ansari Road, Daryaganj
New Delhi - 110002
info@double9books.com
www.double9books.com
Tel. 011-40042856

ABOUT THE AUTHOR

Ruth A. McIntyre is an accomplished historian and writer who specializes in the economic and social history of early America. She holds a Ph.D. in history from the University of Wisconsin-Madison and has published extensively on topics related to colonial America. In "Debts Hopeful and Desperate: Financing the Plymouth Colony," McIntyre draws on her expertise in economic history to provide a detailed account of the financial struggles and successes of the Plymouth Colony. Her meticulous research and analysis provide valuable insights into the economic factors that influenced the development of the colony and the challenges faced by its inhabitants. Her attention to detail and thorough research make "Debts Hopeful and Desperate" an important contribution to the field of early American history and an excellent resource for anyone interested in the economic history of the Plymouth Colony.

CONTENTS

PART I-Financing the Plymouth Colony

The Pilgrims decide to emigrate to America

Of the motives which prompted the founding of New Plymouth, the search of the members of John Robinson's little English congregation at Leyden for an assured religious freedom was certainly the foremost. If this had been their only prospect, it appears that they might have remained in Holland without persecution. They were dissatisfied, however, with their hard economic lot. The most diligent labor brought them little security even in the midst of the prosperous urban life of the Netherlands. There were "fair and beautiful cities flowing with abundance of all sorts of wealth.... Yet it was not long before they saw the grim and ugly face of poverty coming upon them like an armed man, with whom they must buckle and encounter...." The university town of Leyden proved to be "not so beneficial for their outward means of living and estate," yet they "fell to such trades and employments as they best could," until they attained "a competent and comfortable living ... with hard and continual labor."

Most of those who emigrated from Leyden to Plymouth, like their friends who remained behind, were artisans; several performed some operation in clothmaking. William Bradford, for example, was a fustian weaver, Robert Cushman was a wool-comber, and Isaac Allerton, formerly from London, earned his bread as a tailor. Among the handicraftsmen were watchmakers, cabinetmakers, carpenters, and makers of tobacco pipes. Of all who took part in the Plymouth venture, less than a handful had either the experience or capital to be a merchant or, as one might call it, a capitalist. Edward Pickering, who did not take part in the exodus, George Morton, and John Carver, who died in the colony's first year, were exceptions in having trading experience and some means. Two of the leaders with a special competence in theological learning, William Brewster and Edward Winslow, were printers.

As they went about their tasks, respected, yet earning only modest incomes, the members of the English congregation at Leyden worried about their children's future prospects in a foreign country. The young men were "oppressed with their heavy labours" and attracted to soldiering and other occupations their parents considered full of worldly temptation. They also dreaded renewal of the Dutch war with Spain. Deeply aware that they were "men in exile and in a poor condition," they dreamed of a more satisfying life in "those vast and unpeopled countries of America...." Some were eager to take up again the familiar tasks of husbandry and looked forward to acquiring their own houses and land. William Bradford, the historian of Plymouth, asserts that while religious ideals were always basic to the founding of their own community, an economic urge was also behind their fateful decision. Pastor Robinson, on the other hand, feared that in removing to America, his flock would "much prejudice both (their) ... arts and means." **[1]**

They obtain a patent and seek financial backing

The future emigrants now had to make several decisions. First, in what part of the New World should they plant their colony; secondly, how would they defray the heavy costs of shipping stores of food and equipment required for a new settlement? By the time they sent two agents to London in 1617, they had plunged deep into these questions.

Very likely the inexpensive contemporary pamphlets which extolled the benefits of different parts of America helped the leaders at Leyden to fix upon a site. They probably read, for example, the descriptive brochures which the Virginia Company of London had issued in connection with drives to raise money. Robert Harcourt's *A Relation of a Voyage to Guiana* (1614) may have seriously tempted them to put to thè test the fruitful promise of tropical South America, but they were put off by its unhealthy climate. Captain John Smith's tract on New England (1616), which Elder Brewster had in his library at the time of his death, was consulted. Later, the Captain attributed the hardships suffered at Plymouth to the settlers' parsimony in using his "books and Maps ... better cheap" than employing him in person as a guide and counsellor. In the long discussions which preceded any action, it was objected that settling too near the colony at Jamestown ran the risk of Anglican religious persecution; on the other hand, it might be dangerous to be far from help in case the Spaniards, the persistent enemies of English expansion, attacked their infant colony. In the end, "the Lord was solemnly sought in the Congregation by fasting and prayer to direct us ...," and it was decided to plant inside the bounds of Virginia. **[2]**

John Carver and Robert Cushman, trusted members of the group, were the agents selected to approach the political authorities and the Virginia Company in London. They had to negotiate first the delicate matter of how much religious toleration they would be allowed if they went to Virginia.

They sought help from influential friends in the inner circle of the Company. Sir Edwin Sandys and Sir John Wolstenholme intervened with the King and Privy Council to secure approval of a statement of religious beliefs forwarded from Leyden to London. Sandys, a leading colonial promoter, was treasurer of the Company after 1619. As a wealthy merchant, whose financial interests included the colony in Virginia, Wolstenholme was often consulted by the government on commercial matters. Even the good offices of these important men were not enough to win the approval of the royal or ecclesiastical authorities. Not that the King himself, James i, was entirely unfriendly to their plans. In a conversation with his Secretary of State he is reported to have asked how the colony intended to support itself. At the reply, "By fishing," he was said to have exclaimed; "So God have my soul, 'tis an honest trade, 'twas the apostles' own calling." **[3]**

In spite of rebuffs, the agents from Leyden kept trying to secure a patent for land from the Virginia Company. Crushing financial difficulties had recently forced this body to give up underwriting the Virginia colony by a single joint stock. Instead, small groups of associates or partners were authorized to invest in separate stocks for special purposes, such as selling supplies to the settlers. Several groups of partners were also applying to the Company for grants of land they meant to settle at their own expense. In fact, a few such financially independent "private plantations" had already sent over tenants and servants whom they were permitted to direct. It was probably on such terms that the Leyden group hoped to obtain land and to share in its control until the investors were paid off.

At the time of their first application to the Virginia Company the little band of emigrants were depending upon certain "merchants and friends" who had agreed to adventure with them, for the provision of shipping and means. Bradford's obscure chronology makes it puzzling as to who these men were. Writing his *History* much later than the events he described, he seems to place in about February 1620 the offer of support by Thomas Weston they finally accepted, although Weston must have been associated with earlier plans. Several months before, the Virginia Company had already granted them a patent in the name of John Wincob, but the discouragement over the religious negotiations and the state of turmoil in the Virginia Company's management had made some people withdraw their original promise to help. Meanwhile, two members of the Leyden congregation, William Brewster and Thomas Brewer, were in trouble with the English government for illegally publishing some religious tracts. The danger of their capture was disheartening, as was the news about Francis Blackwell, an elder of the English congregation at Amsterdam, who had conducted a group to settle in Virginia. Together with most of his shipmates Blackwell had perished in a vessel so crowded that the 180 passengers were "packed together like herrings." [4]

Some London merchants offer to invest in the colony

Fortunately, there now appeared in Leyden the venturesome fellow countryman whose encouraging new proposals soon gave a lift to low spirits. This was Thomas Weston, a London merchant who had trading interests in the Low Countries. He persuaded the congregation to reject the offers the Dutch West India Company had made to induce them to plant in their territory. He promised, instead, that if the Virginia Company failed to assist, he and his partners would do so.

Weston had served his apprenticeship and been admitted to the Ironmongers Company, one of the London livery companies. A citizen of London, he was altogether a minor figure in the English business world. He engaged in the somewhat hazardous task of selling cloth and other wares to the Low Countries as an "interloper," that is, a trespasser on the tight monopoly the Merchant Adventurers Company of London held there. Although not an investor in Virginia, he evidently shared the fever which was stimulating dreams of profit even in highly speculative colonial ventures, and was willing to shift part of his funds to the relatively untried business of shipping settlers to fish and trade in the New World. It is also likely that he had some sympathy with the religious views of the Leyden group.

For some years Weston's agent at Amsterdam had been Edward Pickering, a merchant married to a member of the Leyden congregation. He had left England for religious reasons and enjoyed a reputation for honesty and success as Weston's factor. Perhaps it was during a routine visit of Weston to his shop in Amsterdam that Pickering informed him of the plans for emigration. None of the leaders at Leyden suspected that in the long run Weston's conduct would not bear out the brisk confidence and easy promises with which he soon persuaded them to accept his promise of assistance. Indeed, in a short time Pickering himself was unable to obtain a proper reckoning of accounts with his employer without returning to England and suing him for a large sum. Weston's finances finally became so crippled by debts, including those to some of the partners in the Plymouth venture, that he left the country and turned to small fishing voyages in New England. [5] This is looking ahead of our story, however.

Weston had come to discern in the colonizing scheme commercial prospects attractive enough to induce several other London businessmen to join in an unincorporated company to send the Leyden congregation overseas. Besides evidence to be presented later that to a certain extent Puritan religious inclination prompted this support, it is likely that the slump in the trade in woolen cloth, the traditional mainstay of English commerce abroad, was also a factor influencing their decision. The disturbance in the course of that trade due partly to its reorganization by the Crown in 1614 helped favor an interest in various new money-making projects. In the rapid growth and dislocation characteristic of early seventeenth-century London relatively few merchants had heard of New England, but Virginia's financial difficulties were well known. Captain John Smith had appealed in 1616 to investors in London and the ports of southwestern England to support colonies to produce profits from the fish and furs of New England. Fishermen, some sent by Londoners, already were sailing off the coast, but Smith recommended settling there so that permanent posts could lengthen the fishing season and permit cargos to be prepared for the arrival of the fleets in the spring. Weston and his partners may have regarded the Pilgrims as the human material to carry out such a plan. Perhaps he suggested planting further north than Jamestown.

Be that as it may, this promoter was welcomed with enthusiasm when he came to confer with Pastor Robinson and to reassure the discouraged that there was no want of shipping or money. The next step was to persuade his Leyden friends to draw up an agreement with his "merchant adventurers," and set forth in black and white the terms under which they would receive aid and he could persuade his fellow-investors to contribute.

1620 – Pilgrims and merchants form a joint stock company

The discussions in England and Leyden over the articles of agreement were protracted. Robert Cushman, as intermediary, thought he closed a hard bargain with the "grasping" merchants. The terms of July 1, 1620, were not unlike those of other colonial enterprises tried in Virginia and Bermuda. The entire capital, including lands, was to be a joint stock fund, divided into shares. Every person over the age of sixteen going to the new colony was rated at £10, and £10 was accounted a single share. Any emigrant outfitting himself with £10 worth of provisions was considered worth £20 or a double share. For example, William Mullins, a well-to-do investor-planter, who died in the first year, left in his will his stock of £40 worth of boots and shoes, expecting it to increase to nine shares at the end of seven years. The adventurers who contributed only money and stayed at home, and the planters, were to continue the joint stock for seven years during which time all profits from "trade, traffic, trucking, working, fishing, or any other means" must remain in the common stock. Then they would divide equally the capital and profits, viz., lands, houses, and goods. The common stock would furnish food, apparel, and provisions.

A good deal of controversy arose when it was learned that the adventurers insisted on harsher terms than those in the original agreement. The assets of the common stock, it was claimed, had not included the houses and home lots of the settlers, nor were they to work seven days a week, two days having been reserved for employment for their own families. The future planters had some right here, for they were the full partners and not the servants of the company. Robert Cushman, who seems to have concealed the stiffer terms, nevertheless vigorously defended them. When criticized by Pastor Robinson, who considered him "... (though a good man and of special abilities in his kind) yet most unfit to deal with other men by reason of his ... too great indifferency for any conditions ...," Cushman retorted to Carver: "... what it is you would have of me I know not; for your crying out, 'Negligence, negligence,' I marvel why so negligent a man was used in the business." If the disheartening new conditions insisted on made many "ready to faint and go back," he could only say that the adventurers, other than Weston, would have withdrawn their help if he had not altered the original ones. With much irritation he objected to the "querimonies and complaints against me, of lording it over my brethren and making conditions fitter for thieves and bondslaves than honest men...." Bradford suggests that Carver never forwarded this heated letter to Leyden, but its indignant tone suggests the vexations which fretted the Pilgrims in their undertaking. **[6]**

The emigrants objected to the new articles and upon arrival in Southampton from Holland rejected Cushman's pleas. This refusal, even though backed by their friends at Leyden and held to until Cushman secured their adherence to the terms in 1621, unfortunately embittered relations with the adventurers. Weston, coming down to Southampton to see them off, "was much offended and told them they must then look to stand on their own legs." Bradford saw in this episode the origin of the "discontent" which later developed between the planters and their chief financial backer.

Despite difficulties and controversy, the colonists set sail

The preparation of the voyage presented practical problems the Pilgrims were ill equipped to solve. The small number who sold their Leyden property to convert it into shipping and stores, had no experience along this line, and their ineptitude made Mr. Weston "merry with our endeavours about buying a ship...." Edward Pickering was the most knowledgeable of them in trade, but his money was not forthcoming, even though Cushman and Weston had expected him to furnish "many hundred pounds." Pastor

Robinson gave voice to pained surprise when he discovered that at the time his flock had turned over the money raised from their scanty possessions, Weston still withheld his own money and had taken absolutely no steps to provide shipping.

The preparations in England bogged down while three purchasing agents scattered their efforts to round up supplies, Cushman in London and Kent, and Carver and Christopher Martin at Southampton. Martin was an Essex man, a newcomer chosen to represent the "strangers" from Essex and London whom the adventurers had recruited to swell the ranks of the planters. He had taken part in settling the terms and was charged with keeping track of matters at Southampton. This was a poor choice, for Martin insulted the Leyden people, whose ways he probably despised. When Cushman later called for an accounting and took up cudgels for the complainers, Martin called them "froward and waspish, discontented people." **[7]**

In spite of all the "clamours and jangling" about the business end of the voyage, there was one important accomplishment during the few anxious months before the *Mayflower* (180 tons) and the *Speedwell* (60 tons) sailed from Southampton on August 5, 1620. Between £1200 and £1600 was raised to cover the expedition's costs. Carver spent £700 of this at Southampton. Unfortunately we do not know how much was supplied by any particular investor. The £50 put in by Martin, Cushman considered insignificant. £500 which the Ferrars, probably John and Nicholas, prominent in the Virginia Company, had promised and then, for some reason, withdrawn, is the only single large investment mentioned. The amount John Carver furnished is not specified, but he was credited by a later writer with having put in most of his considerable substance. With seventy-odd "Gentlemen ... Merchants ... [and] handy craftsmen" subscribing to the partnership, most investments are likely to have been small. At the last minute the party had to sell butter worth £60 to pay off a debt of £100. They left port dangerously short of supplies, a fact which, as Cushman predicted, added to their hardships in the New World.

Their financial difficulties also caused a fateful delay in beginning their voyage. The August departure date was already too late to allow time for crossing the Atlantic and building shelter in mild weather. When the *Speedwell*, leaky and overmasted, forced the ships to put back to land, a score of discouraged passengers withdrew from the voyage. The *Mayflower*, now crowded with the entire group, departed from Plymouth, leaving Robert Cushman behind to serve as chief agent with the adventurers.

Contrary to their patent, the Pilgrims settle at Plymouth

The location where the Pilgrims planned to settle, and their rights to it, were directly related to their future livelihood. Bradford says that when they first made a landfall at Cape Cod they "resolved to stand for the southward ... to find some place about Hudson's River for their habitation." One of the earliest visitors to New Plymouth, John Pory, wrote they had set out for Virginia with letters for the Governor to "give them the best advise he could for trading in Hudson's river." He blamed the master's faulty navigation for bringing them to Cape Cod, where the rough weather of early December forced them to decide not to go southward, but to select a sheltered site nearby. **[8]** This turned out to be New Plymouth.

The Pilgrims carried with them the patent John Peirce, an adventurer we shall meet again, had taken out from the Virginia Company in February 1620. Realizing that it did not apply as far north as New England, the chief colonists drafted the "Mayflower Compact" to avoid disputes over the colony's powers of government. The leaders probably knew before they sailed that the old North Virginia Company had been revived under Sir Ferdinando Gorges as the Council for New England. His grant had been authorized in July 1620 but was not sealed until the *Mayflower* was at sea. If before its departure there was any discussion of heading north, Weston and his associates may have pointed out that later they could solicit a grant from the Council in the Pilgrims' behalf. When the letters with the news of planting at Plymouth reached England the next spring, they promptly secured such a grant. John Peirce was again named as grantee in the indenture, dated June 1, 1621. Its terms permitted Peirce and his associates to lay out 100 acres of land for every person shipped over, and 1500 for public purposes. Besides giving freedom to fish and trade along the coast, it underwrote the colony's authority to make laws. No boundaries were mentioned; a formal patent was expected to specify them at a later date. **[9]**

New Plymouth struggles with hardship and debt

A successful relationship with the partners in England now lay at the heart of the welfare of the infant colony. Even though some of the London businessmen sympathized with the religious aims of the Pilgrims, they expected the investment of their capital to yield a return, and that rather quickly. Promotion of colonial ventures was new and risky. Weston and the later leaders of the merchant adventurers had not learned from the bitter experience of the large, incorporated Virginia Company that a long time must elapse before any profit could be expected from a colonial undertaking. They failed to calculate that even if the colonists engaged promptly in trading furs or catching fish, their initial task must be to build permanent dwellings and to feed themselves and a fair number of women and children. They knew that ships set forth annually by merchants had fished along the New England coast for several years. These usually erected fishing stages and sometimes traded for furs. They required only a modest outlay by the investors in them and wound up their accounts at the end of each voyage. It was much more costly, on the other hand, to uphold a permanent settlement until it was self-sustaining. When even the wealthy backers of Virginia and Bermuda complained about delayed profits, the small group of capitalists supporting the Pilgrims certainly could not afford to sink large funds for supplies year after year without receiving goods in return. At the beginning they apparently underestimated the extent of their task and seem to have neglected consistently the necessary provision for the Plymouth colony.

The urgency of sending returns to these investors pressed on the Pilgrims from the start. When the *Mayflower* sailed home in 1621 without a profitable lading, Weston wrote a sharp criticism to the Governor. He had been informed about how the high death rate and short supplies had weakened the colony during the first dreadful winter, yet he charged the settlers with greater "weakness of judgment than weakness of hands. A quarter of the time you spend in discoursing, arguing and consulting would have done much more.... The life of the business depends upon the lading of this ship, which if you do to any good purpose, that I may be freed from the great sums I have disbursed for the former and must do for the latter [the *Fortune*], I promise you I will never quit the business...."

Robert Cushman, the business agent in England, brought this rebuke from the partners in November 1621. He came in the *Fortune* to inspect the colony briefly and to persuade the colonists to agree to the conditions the adventurers had insisted on. He returned at once to report his findings. The accomplishments of the first year appear in the lively narrative, *Mourt's Relation* or *A Relation of the beginning ... of the English Plantation settled at Plimoth*, printed in 1622. Cushman, George Morton, William Bradford, and Edward Winslow compiled this little tract to encourage the investors about the colony's progress. Although a bit rosy in coloring, it relates what Cushman found.

New Plymouth was situated on a good harbor with plenty of fish and woods close at hand. The settlers had built a fort at the top of the hill and common storehouses containing the first harvest, the colony's precious arsenal and supplies from England. In the small, sturdy, frame houses with roofs of thatch, scattered along the street running up the hill, lived the survivors of the first winter's illness and privation. Their Indian friends, Squanto and Samoset, had helped them conciliate the neighboring Indians and begin trade with them. William Bradford had succeeded Governor Carver, with Isaac Allerton as his assistant. **[10]**

Yet an undercurrent of discontent and friction *Mourt's Relation* did not mention disturbed the settlers. The system of sharing equally in all the arduous labor and what it produced, was one source of unrest. Upon the unloading of thirty-five newcomers sent in the *Fortune* without proper clothing or "so much as a biscuit-cake or any other victuals," the most stout-hearted had a right to murmur at the addition of extra consumers before another crop could be harvested. A gap persisted between the Leyden immigrants and religious exiles, who had ventured their persons and savings, and the London contingent, some of them merely hirelings of the company. Bradford himself wrote Weston about being "yoked with some ill-conditioned people who will never do good...."

Since these strains threatened the successful execution of the conditions with the London backers which he had just persuaded the Pilgrims to sign, Cushman preached a sermon the Sunday before he left on the text, "Let no man seek his own, but every man another's wealth" (1 Corinthians 10:24). Urging his hearers not to labor for self-love or self-profit, he said: "Let there be no prodigal person to come forth and say, Give me the portion of lands and goods that appertaineth to me, and let me shift for myself." No one must think of gathering riches for himself until "our loving friends, which helped us hither, and now again supplied us ...," were paid off. **[11]**

Certainly the leaders of the colony had not been unmindful of their responsibilities to the adventurers. Cushman's ship was freighted with good clapboard and two hogsheads of beaver and otter, a return cargo they judged worth £500. Bad luck assailed them, however, in the first of a series of disasters. A French privateer seized the vessel on its way home and pillaged the returns they had collected with so much effort.

Even so, it is hard for us to understand why the Pilgrims were forced to endure such bitter hardship, indeed, at times, virtual starvation, for a period of about two years after the *Fortune*'s visit. They were continually disappointed at the failure to receive replenishment of their scanty provisions, yet they had to share these with newcomers whose arrival they did not expect. The explanation for these harsh circumstances is to be found not so much in the colony as among the partners in England. The situation was the result of three major events: the defection of Thomas Weston from the ranks of the adventurers; a quarrel with John Peirce over their patent; and the irreparable rift developing inside the partnership itself, which was to precipitate its final dissolution.

Quarrels develop among the London merchants

Up to now Weston had been the Pilgrims' chief supporter in all the business dealings with the London group. He had promised never to fail them if only they signed the onerous terms required by the latter. Before the plundered *Fortune* returned to port, this giver of plausible assurances was the first to desert them. One reason probably was the dispute with his former factor in the Low Countries, Edward Pickering. Near the end of 1621 Pickering left Amsterdam and broke off dealings with Weston. In the suit about accounts connected with their Dutch business, he asserted that Weston owed him hundreds of pounds. A protracted legal wrangle, continued even after Pickering's death and after Weston had departed for New England, revealed the latter's word to be far from reliable. One witness claimed that he heard Weston's brother promise to give some kind of an accounting, not necessarily a true account. Arbitrators investigating the contradictory claims of both parties finally concluded that a matter of some £200 prevented a settlement, but Weston, stubborn and contentious, filed a countersuit against Pickering for a bond of £1500. It seems clear that other adventurers for Plymouth agreed with Pickering in this contest, since John Fowler, James Sherley, and Richard Andrews, as his executors, continued the case after his death.

Weston meanwhile had written Bradford that he disagreed with the rest of the adventurers over their course of action, reproaching them for their "parsimony" in waiting for favorable receipts before they sent provisions. Then he and another stockholder, John Beauchamp, sent out a group of settlers on their own account as a private venture, entirely distinct from the general stock. Weston's men not only brought no victuals for the colony, but relied on the Pilgrims to furnish them necessary shelter and obliged them to dip into their own precious stores of seed corn and salt.

Weston's break with the company in London soon followed. The adventurers held a meeting early in 1622, when the majority agreed to put into the common fund what we might call an additional assessment of one third of their original holding of stock. Those anxious to go on with the business believed it should not be hindered by the laggards, so they resolved to break off the joint stock as soon as the shareowners in the colony should agree. This report of a decision to break up came from Weston and his supporters, but it proved premature, as indeed Bradford suspected so strongly that he did not show their letter to more than a handful of intimates in counsel. Instead, Weston got out. He wrote in April 1622: "I have sold my adventure and debts unto them so as I am quit of you, and you of me...." The company's reaction was that they were "very glad they are freed of him, he being judged a man that thought himself above the general...." Not unrelated to his coming in person to New England in disguise and under an assumed name may have been a large debt he owed the Crown for alum; a Treasury warrant accused him of withdrawing beyond the seas with the purpose of taking his estate after him.

Weston's subsequent projects for colonizing and trading in New England for some time created problems for the settlement at Plymouth. The Pilgrims' leaders more than repaid him for his early support by receiving his men kindly and rescuing his rival colony on Massachusetts Bay from imminent destruction by the Indians. When the promoter himself arrived at their door, virtually destitute, but convincing in his excuses, they fitted him out with enough furs to begin trade again.

Master John Peirce was the next to quarrel with his fellow adventurers in London. A member of the Clothworkers' Company, Peirce claimed that he once employed more than a hundred persons. He was the merchant who had received patents for the Leyden settlers from the Virginia Company in 1620 and later from the Council for New England. He had helped negotiate the terms of agreement between the merchants and the planters. It was under his name that they held the right to take up land around Plymouth. This had made him important enough for Cushman to dedicate *Mourt's Relation* to him. In April 1622, according to the story Bradford told, a version accepted uncritically by many writers, Peirce secretly obtained from the Council for New England a new grant, making the associates hold the lands at Plymouth as his tenants, rather than of the Council. The London adventurers objected and forced him to assign the grant to their Treasurer, now James Sherley, in return for which Peirce demanded £500. The impression is left that Peirce deceived the company and that they were justified in breaking with him.

Peirce, on the other hand, presented his side in a lawsuit in Chancery against Sherley and the other New Plymouth adventurers. It is unfortunate that the answers to the charges do not survive. Peirce claimed an investment of £300 in the colony, reporting that when the adventurers, "being moved by the distressed condition of the Planters ... in that place foreign to them and a vast desert," wished to furnish relief, they couldn't raise the money. At the request of Sherley, Peirce then tried to sustain the plantation by putting up funds to outfit the ill-starred *Paragon*. This vessel, hired from Peirce by the adventurers, sailed twice in the fall and winter of 1622–23 with freight and passengers, chiefly women and children. When wintry seas forced her to turn back the second time, Peirce said that, although the adventurers had promised that he should not suffer any losses from the voyage, contrary to such agreement, he bore the entire loss. After Peirce was unable to refit his ship at Portsmouth quickly enough to suit the adventurers, the latter sent a writ from Admiralty to arrest him for £600. Under his brother Richard's bond, the merchant returned to London, where the adventurers "made a great clamour against ... [him] for some supposed unjust dealing...." They attempted to buy out his indenture, ultimately succeeding in obtaining from Peirce's brother a £500 bond to deliver it. This compelled Peirce to sign it over to Sherley; besides he lost the chance to recoup his loss by another voyage. In spite of a complex series of legal maneuvers (Bradford wrote that Peirce "sued them in most of the chief courts in England ... [and] brought it to the Parliament"), he was unable to regain his investment and reported that he suffered such inconvenience and damaged reputation that he emerged a poor man.

While John Peirce held the title to the Plymouth lands "in trust," he seems to have acted within his legal rights in his maneuver to exchange the indenture of 1621 for a new patent, but his purpose in doing so without informing his associates in London and New Plymouth is not clear. It evidently so angered them that when they found out they stubbornly refused to settle with him and pay the £500 fee he demanded. They probably were not unwilling to ruin him. Bradford, on the other hand, gave short shrift to the fact that the *Paragon* sailed at Peirce's charge and clearly accepted the opinion of the adventurers that God had directed her mishaps against him because of his action on the patent. **[13]**

The joint stock company breaks up

Meanwhile the most active of the remaining adventurers had determined to forget the fiasco of the *Paragon* and prepared two vessels, the *Anne* and the *Little James*, to carry a "large and liberal" supply and a contingent of passengers intending to settle. Both arrived in Plymouth in the summer of 1623. A great part of the adventurers' hope for profit rested in the *Little James*, a small pinnace built to remain in the colony for its use. Bradford said "the adventurers did overpride themselves in her," for her troubles began even on the way over. Because her commission allowed her to capture prize vessels, when the captain failed to seize a French vessel, the crew became "rude" and mutinous, claiming they were hired on shares for privateering, and not for employment in fishing or trade. Before they would sail on colony business, Bradford was obliged to negotiate wage contracts with them. The *Little James'* first voyage to the Narragansett country returned without success, because she was not equipped with trading goods to match what the Dutch could offer the Indians. A series of calamities assailed her; she lost her mast, and later, through negligence, sank off the Maine coast. The loss of this voyage and the cost of raising her came to about £400 or £500. In the next step of her unhappy career, she was seized on her return to England by one of the adventurers for a debt owed him by the others. **[14]**

Emmanuel Altham, the *Little James'* captain, himself an adventurer, expressed the hopes of the English businessmen for the little plantation. He had observed the efforts of the "honest men" of Plymouth to "do, in what lies in them, to get profit to the adventurers," and he anticipated that fishing voyages, collection of beaver, as well as of timber, were all ways of raising their returns. Yet he warned those back home that provisions for twelve months at least were needed to allow the settlers time for building houses and making a success of these different enterprises. **[15]**

New Plymouth at first had expected to engage in fishing, by now the source of successful returns to many small West Country merchants whose ships were cruising up and down the New England coast and then carrying dried fish to market in southern Europe. The colony's most ambitious attempt in this direction did, indeed, secure a patent for Cape Ann from Lord Sheffield, taken in the names of Robert Cushman and Edward Winslow. Yet the hope that the Pilgrims "could fall once into the right course" for profitable fishing and saltmaking proved unfounded. The first fishing season was a failure; the boatmaker died; the saltmaker turned out to be incompetent. The colony almost lost to rivals the fishing stage erected on Cape Ann. Even the title to the land had flaws in it. In short, this ended "that chargeable business" and added only bitterness to the adventurers' cup. **[16]**

The seven-year partnership between the London adventurers and the planters at Plymouth, unless renewed, as once had been suggested, was to end about 1627 or 1628. In fact, the succession of blighted hopes and dissensions just described dissolved it earlier. Several innovations prepared the way for a new arrangement satisfactory both to the colonists and to their English supporters.

After two harvests the colony itself had decided that the task of raising food for the settlers would prosper only if it was separated from that of earning profits for London. In 1623 a parcel of land was allotted to each man to till for his family and to maintain those who were exempt from agricultural employment because of other duties. In abandoning the "common course and condition" everyone worked harder and more willingly. The food problem was ended, and after the first abundant harvest under individual cultivation, the Pilgrims did not have to endure the meager rations of the first years. The plots assigned them permanently in 1624 became privately owned in 1627. Three heifers and a bull sent over by the adventurers in response to Bradford's request throve and multiplied, so there was cattle to be divided among the households when the general stock was terminated. **[17]**

The alliance between the London adventurers and the colony began to crack as early as 1623, when several men arrived in Plymouth "upon their own Particulars." This meant they were not financed by the joint stock and thus had no share in the land or profits common to the company; they were also free from employment for the common good. John Oldham and his associates, arriving in the *Anne*, were the first. Those of the "particulars" who accepted Bradford's terms and stayed soon displayed jealousy over the details providing for their inclusion as members of the colony. The Reverend John Lyford, a Puritan clergyman sent over by the adventurers, probably to restrain the Separatist tendency of the Pilgrims, succeeded in fanning to flame the friction smoldering among the colonists who held different religious views. While Bradford's scathing condemnation of Lyford is clearly biased, it must be admitted that the minister was a malcontent and hypocrite, to specify some of his more mentionable sins. He and Oldham secretly wrote letters full of disgruntled complaints to the company about how things were run. For example, the "particulars" disliked their exclusion from the fur trade and the restrictions giving them so small a voice in government. Fortunately, Bradford intercepted their letters and held them until the elements of ferment gave rise to a public display of the Oldham-Lyford opposition. The Governor skillfully suppressed the dissidents, but when Lyford's friends among the adventurers in England heard about it, their distrust of the Pilgrims' independent religious polity boiled over into indignation. Other controversial issues, such as whether to send

Pastor Robinson to join his flock in Plymouth, coming together with all the financial losses, now brought about such a gaping chasm in the company that it "broke in pieces." [18]

One group of the adventurers, led by Treasurer Sherley, remained sympathetic to the Pilgrims and wrote that they did not care whether the colony yielded worldly riches, provided it was rich in grace and walking with God. Sherley, especially, defended it against the charges of waste and inefficiency brought by its attackers. Perhaps he made allowances based on the same information as reported by Emmanuel Altham that "the burden lieth on the shoulder of some few who are both honest, wise and careful. And if it were not for them few, the plantation would fall, and come to nothing—yea, long before this time...." Altham blamed the company for sending over so many helpless people and for the fact that the planters had not enough "good trucking stuff to please the Indians."

When the dissolution took place, Sherley reported as the chief reason "the many crosses and losses and abuses by sea ... which have caused us ... so much charge, and debts ... as our estates ... were not able to go on without impoverishing ourselves, and much hindering if not spoiling our trades and callings...." Even the faction deserting on the pretense of Brownism in the colony, suffered from the same want of money which was "such a grievous sickness now-a-days ... that it makes men rave and cry out...." [19] He referred, of course, to the depressed economic conditions carried over into the reign of Charles i.

The Pilgrims agree to purchase the merchants' interests in the company

It took two years of negotiations before the adventurers agreed with Isaac Allerton to accept the following terms for winding up the old stock. They signed them in London on November 16, 1626. Then, reluctantly but courageously, the members of the colony known as the "Undertakers" pledged their own credit to carry them out. The forty-two adventurers signing the composition in London [20] consented to sell to their associates in New Plymouth all the shares of the stock in the lands or merchandise up to now belonging to them both. The "generality" in Plymouth in turn undertook to pay £1800 in annual installments of £200 each, to be paid at the west side of the Royal Exchange in London, beginning in September 1628. The five merchants designated to receive the payments were John Pocock, John Beauchamp, Robert Keane, Edward Bass, and James Sherley. The Pilgrims also assumed £600 remaining of the debts of £1400 which Sherley reported the company owed in 1624. How this compared as a return with the original sums invested in the plantation at Plymouth, we do not know. Captain John Smith reported in 1624 that altogether £7000 had been spent, and it has been suggested that £5600 of this was share capital, and £1400 debts, so that in repaying £1800 the colony was giving back to the London adventurers only one third of the share capital. **[21]**

The London investors were linked by common associations

As we move beyond the period dominated by the company of merchant adventurers, how are we to characterize this group? What was their usual form of business, and had they other colonial interests besides Plymouth? Did they sympathize with the religious aims of the emigrants, or were they simply indifferent to them as long as profits beckoned? Captain John Smith's statement that Plymouth was financed by "... about 70. some Merchants, some handy-crafts men, some adventuring great sums, some small, as their estates and affections served," is revealing, but to discover answers to these questions requires close analysis of the names of the individual subscribers.

> This is the complete list of merchants known to have invested in the Colony. It includes the signers of the composition of 1626 as Bradford recorded them in his Letterbook, and, in brackets, five other persons. Names have been rearranged alphabetically. Spellings follow Bradford.

Robert Allden
Emm. Alltham
Richard Andrews
Thomas Andrews
Lawrence Anthony
Edward Bass
John Beauchamp
Thomas Brewer
Henry Browning
William Collier
[Christopher Coulson]
Thomas Coventry
Thomas Fletcher
Thomas Goffe
[William Greene]
Peter Gudburn
Timothy Hatherley
Thomas Heath
William Hobson
Robert Holland
Thomas Hudson

Robert Kean
Eliza Knight
John Knight
Myles Knowles
John Ling
Thomas Millsop
Thomas Mott
Fria. Newbald
[John Peirce]
William Penington
William Penrin
[Edward Pickering]
John Pocock
Daniel Poynton
William Quarles
John Revell
Newman Rookes
Samuel Sharp
James Sherley
John Thorned
Matthew Thornhill
Joseph Tilden
Thomas Ward
[Thomas Weston]
John White
Richard Wright

If Smith's figure of seventy is correct, the survival of a partial list of subscribers is a handicap, for about one third are completely unknown. Thomas Weston, John Peirce, Edward Pickering, Christopher Coulson, and William Greene should be added to the list. A little less than half have been identified as London merchants, but their major contribution to the Colony's support entitles them to close inspection. John White was a Puritan lawyer in London, while Emmanuel Altham belonged to a family of landed gentry. Many names are so obscure that it has not proved practicable to seek them out. It may be inferred, however, that the nonmercantile adventurers included some with background in a craft, such as that of the printer, Thomas Brewer. At the time of the *Mayflower*'s expedition most of the sponsors were relatively young and attained maturity during the two or three decades after 1620, when some became prominent in the City and in the parliamentary opposition to Charles i.

Just as the threads in a tapestry vary in color, but the pattern of the weave repeats itself, so with the detailed circumstances of the careers of the adventurers. Most of those we know belonged to one of London's livery companies and were citizens. They held company or City offices; some were listed in a particular ward as wealthy enough to be noted by

Crown officials as men of substance. One rose to the important role of Lord Mayor. The merchants were engaged in foreign trade and kept a shop or place of business in the heart of London. The crowded, narrow streets and lanes adjoining the widest thoroughfare, Cheapside, or close to the river, near London Bridge, then "replenished on both sides with fair and beautiful buildings, inhabitants for the most part rich merchants," were their surroundings. They met to settle debts and accounts in the arcades of the handsome building of the Royal Exchange in Cornhill or in one of the taverns. The shipowners among them said goodbye to their captains from the wharves lining the Thames, the famous waterway connecting London with the sea. Some traveled on business to the Netherlands. The members of companies could attend meetings and feasts in a well-appointed hall, such as the Goldsmiths' in Foster Lane, or on occasion one of the great banquets the Lord Mayor gave at the Guildhall. They worshiped in the numerous parish churches, and doubtless others, besides Robert Keane, often heard lecturers or noted Puritan preachers, such as Hugh Peter. Sherley and Beauchamp, at least, had an additional residence across the river in Surrey; others held lands at some distance from the City. Like all merchants of their time, they were apt to have connections with the gentry; Thomas Andrews was himself knighted by Cromwell for service to the parliamentary cause.

Thomas Andrews, in fact, was one of the most notable merchants attached to the Puritan and parliamentary cause in the English Civil Wars. Although not a member of an older family of wealth, he succeeded in acquiring riches and a leading role in politics and finance under the Commonwealth and Protectorate. In 1638 he became master of the Leathersellers, his company. A share in collecting customs revenue for the Crown provided him with what was usually a profitable investment. Subsequently, he served the City as alderman and arrived at the pinnacle of office as Lord Mayor in 1649. At the beginning of the conflict with the King, this ambitious merchant served on the City's all-important Militia Committee, which, besides controlling London forces, was "largely responsible for organizing money for the parliamentary army." One of the committees he served as treasurer, collected about £1,000,000. He helped manage money raised for putting down the Irish Rebellion and by selling lands confiscated from the King and Royalists. Andrews himself contributed huge sums to the parliamentary forces. Both Edward Winslow, a Plymouth colonist, and James Sherley were his fellow members on other commissions, one to judge treasons against the Commonwealth and the other to dismiss ministers and schoolmasters thought to be "insufficient," i.e., not conforming to Puritan standards. In the later political struggle between the Independents and Presbyterians, Andrews belonged to the Independent party. It is difficult to explain in a short space how these groups differed about church government and politics. Roughly speaking, an English Independent developed ideas of religious toleration, self-government for each congregation, and opposition to a state church, which were rejected by Presbyterians. New Englanders, on the other hand, enforced the congregational form of church government. It is probable that a London merchant who had arrived at the position of Independency by the 1640s would have sympathized earlier with the religious views of the settlers of New England.

Andrews' business interests were widely scattered in trade, colonization, land speculation, and finance. He joined the effort of the Massachusetts Bay Company to found a Puritan refuge in New England; he agreed to lend it £25 and later became one of a group of "Undertakers" who took over its debts in 1634. In the 1640s he had a crucial role in financing new trades pioneered by the East India Company. As a director of that Company for many years, he was required to own at least £1000 of stock. At one time he invested in a rival syndicate which traded on the Malabar Coast of India; another of its schemes was to plant a colony on the West Coast of Africa. Eventually, Andrews came to co-operate with the Company and rose to be its governor. **[22]** These varied mercantile enterprises, and they could be extended into land dealings, suggest that the young Thomas Andrews was induced to support the Plymouth venture by calculations of profit as well as initial approval of its religious aims.

On the whole, however, the religious bonds of the London backers of Plymouth Colony have received too little attention and their mercenary objectives have been contrasted too sharply with the purity of motive of the Pilgrims. In the Massachusetts Bay Company, on the other hand, it is acknowledged that the investors shared "Puritan" religious and political ends inspiring them to encourage colonial ventures. This company included among its members nine Londoners who previously had been adventurers in the founding of Plymouth. These were Richard Andrews, Thomas Andrews, just described, Christopher Coulson, Thomas Goffe, Robert Keane, John Pocock, John Revell, Samuel Sharpe, and John White. **[23]** Let us glance at the background of each and consider its relation to his participation in both plantation schemes.

Richard Andrews persisted in a business career rather than sharing the prominence of his brother in government affairs. He remained interested in Plymouth even after 1626, becoming a partner with the "Undertakers." Thus, he certainly was not one of the adventurers whom Treasurer Sherley described as offended by the Colony's form of religious worship. His enthusiasm for New England extended to Massachusetts Bay. He, too, lent it money and entered the syndicate of those who furnished supplies after 1634. He was a member of the Haberdashers' Company, a renowned sponsor of Puritan preachers. His business was conducted at the sign of the Mermaid near the Cross in Cheapside; this was a well-known tavern in Bread Street with an entrance from Cheapside. Late in the 1620s he owned shares in the ships *Rebecca* (200 tons), the *Jane* (200 tons), and the *Roebuck* (80 tons), all of which received letters of marque to capture pirates. Another of his ships prepared to undertake a voyage to Massachusetts early in 1645. Most of his trading probably was with the Netherlands, where in 1632 his factor ran afoul of Sir Paul Pindar, a wealthy merchant who shared in collecting customs revenue and was privileged to hold a patent for alum. Andrews and the factor were charged with bringing in some alum contrary to Pindar's patent. In the 1640s Andrews spent several years in Rotterdam, where there was a trading center of the Merchant Adventurers; he may have been a member of that organization selling English cloth abroad. Andrews' search for profit doubtless helped direct him to invest in New England, but his gifts to the poor and to the ministers of Massachusetts substantiate John Winthrop's claim that the donor was a "godly man," consistently dedicated to Puritan causes. He even sent a gift to the Indians to be distributed by John Eliot and Thomas Mayhew. This included "8 little books against swearing," "3 books against drunkenness," and "2 dozen of small books called the rule of the New Creature," all summoning up Puritan themes. **[24]**

Christopher Coulson was named in Peirce's suit as an assistant of the New Plymouth Company, but he had withdrawn before the composition. While deciding not to participate in Isaac Allerton's investment in the Maine fur trade, he did become an assistant of the Bay Company. Coulson was a dyer of cloth. As one of the well-to-do citizens of Dowgate Ward, he served on the City's Common Council and, with Thomas Andrews, on the Militia Committee. **[25]**

Too deep an involvement in colonial ventures was likely to harm one's credit. The first deputy governor and treasurer of the Massachusetts Bay Company, Thomas Goffe, sank into heavy debt for a time, part contracted for Winthrop personally and part for the Company. Goffe complained bitterly when, in a difference with Winthrop, he received no payment. As a shipowner with a share in the *Welcome* and in two other vessels which seem to have crossed the Atlantic, he wrote that his shipowning was far from successful in 1630, the year of the initial Winthrop voyage. His affairs were "in an ambiguous and desperate estate" until some of his creditors, pitying him, took over part of the plantation debts and lent him enough capital to begin trading again. Though he suffered financial loss from the Puritan venture in Massachusetts, Goffe perhaps derived a greater measure of satisfaction from his donation to another Puritan cause. Along with a number of other Londoners he supported a daily lecture at the Church of St.

Antholin's. This afforded Puritan ministers and lecturers a platform for their views until the government suppressed the society, known as the Feoffees of Impropriations, which had been active in raising money to encourage a preaching ministry in London and elsewhere. **[26]**

By investing in the Pilgrims' colony, John Pocock began what was a long association with New England. John Peirce called this merchant a leader in its support, and even after the composition Pocock extended it credit. Recruited as an officer in the Bay Company, he continued his generosity to that colony for about a quarter of a century. In fact, after Thomas Weld and Hugh Peter had concluded a mission in England in Massachusetts' behalf, Pocock succeeded them as London agent; he also offered his shop in Watling Street, where he conducted business as a merchant taylor and woolen draper, to exhibit their disputed accounts. A fifteen years' wait for payment of about £150 worth of cloth he had sent in 1641 to assist Massachusetts, did not deter him from investing substantially in John Winthrop Jr.'s project for establishing ironworks at Braintree, Massachusetts. Pocock fully sympathized with Puritanism and the parliamentary opposition to the King, as demonstrated by his contributions to the St. Antholin's lectureship and his inclusion among the promoters of the London scheme to raise money for troops to help crush the Irish Rebellion. Parliament next made him one of the officials to whom were entrusted the Anglican church revenues so that they might be converted to the use of new Puritan preachers. **[27]** John Pocock's range of activities indicates that he, too, looked kindly on Plymouth and Massachusetts Bay as outposts of Puritan influence.

Three of the merchants who had subscribed to the Plymouth venture, Robert Keane, John Revell, and Samuel Sharpe, actually emigrated to Massachusetts. The first to come over was Samuel Sharpe, who arrived in Salem as a member of the council chosen to assist Governor Endecott and to serve as business agent for the merchant, Matthew Cradock. In fact, Sharpe carried over the copy of the Company's new patent. Had Endecott died, he was one of two designated to take over the government of the colony. Sharpe settled in Salem and became a freeman in 1632. **[28]**

John Revell's part in financing the early Bay venture was clearly more important, however. Not only was he an assistant of the Massachusetts Bay Company, but he took a one-sixteenth share in a large ship for the transport of passengers and supplies to New England the Company could not afford. He also contributed £40 for freight during preparation for the 1630 fleet of vessels. He came aboard Winthrop's vessel for dinner during the crossing, returning to his own under the salute of a volley of three shots. It is not known why he returned to England after a few weeks. He must have planned to stay, as his wife and children were with him. Back in London he belonged to the group of "Undertakers" supplying the Massachusetts plantation. [29]

The mind and temper of the final emigrant, Robert Keane, is clearer to us than that of any other adventurer in New Plymouth, with the possible exception of James Sherley. No career could illustrate better the compatibility of a calculated design to add to one's wealth in the New World with the satisfaction of a sensitive Puritan conscience. At the same time that he was improving his worldly estate in London and Boston, Keane was walking the paths of salvation, he hoped, leaving in the interesting document, his last will and testament, a full discussion of both objectives. His account books, numerous as they were, can hardly have exceeded in bulk the handwritten ledgers he filled with comments on Scriptural books and on the sermons he had heard. In London, he laboriously noted in 1627 and 1628 the contents of discourses in several churches, including the famed St. Stephen's, Coleman Street, where he listened to Mr. John Davenport, and one at Hackney visited by Master Hugh Peter. He attended some of the lectures at St. Antholin's but most often, service at what he calls "Cornhill," probably either St. Michael, Cornhill, or St. Peter's, Cornhill. Between attending several services a month and writing down what was said, he gave a good deal of earnest thought to religion.

In his business career, Keane asserted that he was "self-made," with no inheritance from his father. After apprenticeship in the Merchant Taylors' Company, he took a shop in Birchin Lane, a street where the sellers of clothing displayed their wares. Either because of his fortunate marriage to the daughter of a gentleman or, more likely, because of success in business which enabled him to accumulate an estate of some £2000 or £3000, he enjoyed the modest rewards of a prosperous citizen, such as membership in the Honourable Artillery Company of London. His routine business included supplying liveries for the pages and footmen of the Lord Chamberlain. Keane was associated with James Sherley and the other merchants who furnished Plymouth with capital and direction. With Sherley he signed a letter to the colonists in 1624, and Peirce mentions him as an "assistant." In the list of 1626, Keane was among the five designated to receive the £1800 to be paid by the Colony. In the Massachusetts Bay Company he was one of the inner ring of "Undertakers." Keane was also the leading spirit in the organization of the Ancient and Honorable Artillery Company of Massachusetts. He served as the first captain of this military company, the earliest to be chartered in America.

The religious pressures upon a conscience like Keane's are unmistakable, for amidst all the troubles he suffered in Massachusetts he described the new commonwealth, in its closeness to the Gospel, as little different from that which had summoned him to leave England in 1635. Of those who came to Boston, he was remarkable for his wealth and his successful application of it to new kinds of profitable transactions, such as investment in land and trade to Bermuda or the West Indies. In time, he installed his son, Benjamin, in Birchin Lane in London to act as his agent and to sell cloaks. Keane's career is a model of the intertwining of "merchandise, reading and writing," all matters of importance to Puritans anxious to redeem their time on earth. **[30]**

Most London Puritans whose interests embraced first Plymouth and then Massachusetts Bay were merchants, but one was a prominent lawyer of the Middle Temple. This was "Counsellor" John White, so called to distinguish him from the minister, John White of Dorchester, another leader in New England colonization. The lawyer John White became an investor in the latter's enterprise, the Dorchester Company. Many activities mark him as a sympathizer with nonconformity, but his record with the New Plymouth venture suggests that he was one of the adventurers opposed to Separatism. While these were debating hotly the treatment Bradford had meted out to Lyford, partly for his use of the Book of Common Prayer, the faction favoring Lyford chose John White to be moderator in their interest. On terminating his interest in Plymouth in 1626, he perhaps was the lawyer John Peirce chose to arbitrate in his behalf in the course of his lawsuit against the adventurers. By becoming one of the Lay Feoffees, a group of trustees raising money to support the preachers they favored in the churches, White lent his name to one of the most dangerous of the Puritan efforts to oppose the policy of strict conformity insisted on by English authorities. He attended meetings of the early Massachusetts Bay Company and perhaps at one time contemplated emigration to New England, as suggested by one of John Winthrop's correspondents. Remaining in London, he became a strong influence instead in settling such difficult problems as whether the prospective emigrants or the London merchants were to control the joint stock. A friend of Winthrop wrote in 1640 of this consistent friend of Massachusetts: "... there is so little money stirring to be exc[h]anged for the Plantation and so many hands to catch for it, that there is no hopes of obtaining any ... nor of Mr. White the Lawyer ... it being disposed some other way...." John White's greatest service to Puritanism and the parliamentary cause came when he was chosen to serve for Southwark in the Long Parliament. There he presided over two committees, one to replace "scandalous" ministers with Puritan preachers, and the other to care for ministers who had been "plundered" by the preceding government. A little of the affectionate regard in which he was held may be observed in that when he died in 1645, the House of Commons accompanied his body to Middle Temple Church for burial. **[31]**

So much for the investors in both the New England colonies. What we know of the other New Plymouth adventurers does not contradict the sketch set forth of men of moderate prosperity or wealth, Puritan in religious outlook, and usually of some prominence in the City's affairs in the period of the Civil Wars. It remains to discuss more fully the two merchants who, along with Richard Andrews, did most to maintain the credit of the Plymouth "Undertakers" after 1627. These were John Beauchamp and James Sherley.

A member of the Salters' Company, Beauchamp was an early associate of Thomas Weston, with whom he furnished the *Sparrow*, a small vessel sent to Plymouth on private account in 1622. Like Weston he had traded as an "interloper" to the Low Countries from about 1612 to 1619. In the composition, Beauchamp was one of the five chosen to receive payment of the settlement money, and Sherley requested that he be joined with him as agent or factor in London for the "Undertakers." Another New England colonial interest of his was the Muscongus patent in which Edward Ashley served as agent in fur trade with the Indians. The merchant also had a share in at least one ship which received a commission to take pirates. About 1640 he was judged to be not among the first, but the third, rank of citizens able to contribute to the King's financial needs. Beauchamp lent money to various persons and apparently was rigorous in collection, for even Sherley described him as "somewhat harsh," while a debtor's widow, suing him, accused him of "unconscionably" prosecuting her at law after her husband had discharged his debt to him. This appears to be in character with the attitude we shall see he assumed in the winding up of the Pilgrims' debts. **[32]**

James Sherley's career is indeed the central one among the London merchant supporters of the colony at Plymouth. In December 1624, when he was thought to be fatally ill, his generosity was called "the only glue of the company." Without his "unfeigned love" for the Pilgrims, his patience and willingness to disregard the harsh judgments of the dissatisfied adventurers, it was said that the project would have failed.

Sherley was apprenticed to his father, Robert Sherley, as a goldsmith in 1604, and became a full member of the Goldsmiths' Company in 1612. Like several other members of his family he remained in close association with the Company throughout his life, although it is clear that he did not follow the craft of making plate or objects of gold and silver. Instead, he was in trade. Yet he was first active in Company business through his collection of Company rents, and he was chosen to take part in the ceremonial occasions of the Goldsmiths. On Lord Mayor's Day, 1633, attired in a rich livery gown "furred with Foynes," Sherley appeared at dinner at the Guildhall to "welcome the Lords Ladies & other guests." On another occasion, before dining with members of a neighboring company, he joined them in a special service at St. Mary Woolnoth's. Beginning with the office of assistant, and refusing the third wardenship in 1639, he had risen to the Company's highest office, that of prime warden, by 1644. In this capacity he attended frequent wardens' and court meetings and presided over a complex amount of Company business involving leases, loans, relations to the Mint, and other matters. Goldsmiths' Hall, in Foster Lane, was a busy center for financial transactions.

Sherley's own London address is something of a puzzle. Letters were directed to him in 1623 both as "dwelling on London bridge at the Golden hoospyte," and to Crooked Lane. His brother John had a shop on London Bridge; perhaps in early years they shared a dwelling among the fine merchants' houses erected there. Crooked Lane was a winding artery in Candlewick Ward, the site of a noted Dutch tavern; this may have been where James Sherley maintained his business address. Like many others who had left the stench, noise, and possible plague of London, he later had a home in Clapham, Surrey, then a rural environment. He wrote Bradford of carrying his records there in 1636 when the plague was raging in London.

It was from Clapham that Sherley was chosen to serve in the public capacities then filled by men of substance. He was a member of the Surrey committee for levying assessments for the militia. In confirmation of the strong religious tendency evident in his correspondence with Bradford, he was an elder in the Croydon Classis in Surrey, formed during a reorganization of the English Church along Presbyterian lines. The New England Company, erected to spread the Gospel to the Indians, included him among its members. Parliament made him one of a Surrey group appointed in 1652 to deal with the problem of supplying proper ministers and schoolmasters in the churches of his county. His son was granted the right to administer his will in Clapham in 1657. **[33]**

Early in his business career Sherley very likely was connected with the Netherlands trade, for he was sufficiently friendly with Edward Pickering, Weston's agent, who died in 1623, to be one of the executors of his will; in 1630 he wrote that he had spent nearly three months in Holland. In underwriting the Plymouth "Undertakers," he perhaps was committed financially as deeply as he could afford, for he did not join the Massachusetts Bay Company. He did own ships in the New England trade, however, one of which was hired by Isaac Allerton. He had a share in the Ashley scheme in Maine and in voyages to Massachusetts Bay. The latter colony owed him money in 1648. **[34]**

Nothing has been discovered about the remaining adventurers to alter the character of the group as described above; they were chiefly Puritan merchants, possessed of substantial means but not great wealth. It is true that Robert Alden, a prosperous salter, at the opening of the Civil Wars adhered to the Royalist minority of London citizens. William Greene, described as "one of the most religious of the adventurers," was among those whose opposition to sending out any more emigrants from Leyden, made him withdraw his support. Another, Thomas Brewer, lumped together and imprisoned by the royal authorities with Brownists, by 1640 had become Anabaptist, a sect not tolerated by the Pilgrims._**[35]**_ For the most part, however, a consistency of business, religious, and political purposes seems to have prevailed among those who closed out the Company of Adventurers to New Plymouth.

PART II-Plymouth Reorganizes Financially

The colony looks to the fur trade to pay its debts

The method devised for repaying what was a stiff debt for the young colony, as one writer puts it, "shows considerable business ingenuity." With ownership transferred from London to Plymouth, the plantation became a virtual corporation in fact. Two important matters still had to be decided. Should all the settlers share in the disposition of the corporate lands and assets and in the obligation of repayment to the adventurers? How would they be able to guarantee satisfaction of the London men? It was wisely decided to include as holders of shares, or "purchasers," all men, whatever their former status, who were either heads of families or single and not indentured servants. At the 1627 division of assets in the form of land and cattle, every such person received twenty acres of tillable land to add to the one-acre portion allotted him when the plantation had ended the "common course." The livestock was parceled out for a time among twelve groups, a total of 156 individuals, with every six persons receiving one cow and two goats. These "purchasers," of whom in 1640 fifty-three were listed as living in Plymouth and five in England, were to benefit from subsequent divisions of land as the colony opened up.

The immediate task of paying the Londoners fell upon a group of eight leaders, including William Bradford, Miles Standish, Isaac Allerton, Edward Winslow, William Brewster, John Howland, John Alden, and Thomas Prence, known as the "Undertakers." These men founded a partnership to manage the fur trade of the colony for six years, the time during which the returns from the Pilgrims' most profitable business enterprise were to be devoted to paying the debt and importing essential English goods. This became the business of the eight who took possession at once of the company boats and "the whole stock of furs, fells, beads, corn, wampampeak, hatchets, knives, &c."

It may be asked why the "Undertakers" were willing to saddle themselves with such a responsibility. The answer is their sense of obligation to their old friends in Leyden, as well as their fidelity to the London merchants. Most of the former adventurers had so opposed sending over any more people from Leyden that the beloved Pastor Robinson prophetically, before his death, looked for no further help until means came from Plymouth itself. The first example of such aid would cost the partnership £500, the amount paid for the emigration in 1629 of what was a welcome but "weak" addition to the colony.

Three London merchants agree to continue as Plymouth's partners

It was extremely important to tap resources of English credit to secure new working capital for the trade. It might have to be borrowed at rates as high as 30–50%, instead of the 6–8% Sherley reported as current for English business loans in 1628. This explains why Allerton was sent to London to persuade the former treasurer of the company, Sherley, and others in England to join the "Undertakers" as partners. Together with Sherley, John Beauchamp and Richard Andrews consented to the proposal. One immediate result was that Sherley forebore collection of £50 he had lent at 30% two years earlier, and induced John Beauchamp and Richard Andrews to do the same for goods they had provided while the negotiations were in progress. At Bradford's request, Sherley and Beauchamp were designated as factors to receive the furs shipped to London, while Allerton, long since Bradford's right hand as chief of the assistants in the colony, continued to act as business agent of the "Undertakers." **[36]**

The Pilgrims encounter difficulties in the fur trade

Under skillful and energetic management the Plymouth traders soon succeeded in expanding their collection of pelts from the Indians. The trade in furs had begun in 1621, when Squanto guided the Pilgrims' shallop to the Massachusetts Indians. Unluckily, the first return to England of two hogsheads, estimated to be worth about £400, was captured in the *Fortune*. In fact, a considerable quantity of what was collected in the first years never reached England at all and thus produced no credit for the colony. Instead, Weston's malice was all they got for 170 pounds of beaver lent him on his arrival in 1623. Another part of their precious hoard of skins paid some fishermen for raising the *Little James*, while Turkish pirates seized an additional 800 pounds on its way to England in 1625. Finally, the colony purchased with beaver about £500 worth of trading goods, including Biscay rugs, from a wrecked ship they learned was for sale at Monhegan.

After the joint stock company had broken up, Standish took £277 worth of beaver with him to pay Sherley. A large haul of 700 pounds was the result of a single autumn voyage to the Kennebec, purchased, remarkably enough, with home-grown corn. No lack of energy on the part of the Plymouth traders had prevented returns, but scarcity of the kind of English trading goods, such as hatchets, knives, and trading cloth, which the Indians wanted. In the early stages such goods had to be bought from passing vessels. On at least one occasion valuable coat beaver, which Bradford expected to bring about 20s. per pound in England, was sold to these at 3s. a pound, in exchange for beads and knives.

As the "Undertakers" took over management, it was evident that numerous competing trading posts, settled up and down the New England coast, were beginning to cut into Plymouth's sources of fur and to raise the price the Indians demanded for it. The scapegrace, Thomas Morton of Merrymount, in particular, aroused their ire by selling the natives the forbidden articles, liquor, guns, and powder. On top of this, his introduction of such pastimes as setting up a May Pole and "drinking and ... dancing and frisking together" with Indian maidens so seriously offended their religious sensibilities that they sent Captain Standish to evict Morton in 1628.

In the early stages of the fur trade, transportation presented considerable difficulty. Shallops or open boats were used at first, but a small vessel was needed to coast in and out of the little harbors for several weeks at a time, carrying a few traders and their supplies. To provide for this, an ingenious house carpenter lengthened one of the shallops and built a deck, affording a hold for long voyages in the winter. **[37]**

The "Undertakers" now decided to build a pinnace on the Manomet River, twenty miles south of Plymouth, and to erect there a permanent trading house of hewn oak planks, furnished with trading goods and in the care of two men the year round. Aptucxet was the name of their first post; it was located so strategically in relation to Buzzard's Bay that its site is at the edge of the modern passage, the Cape Cod Canal. In the seventeenth century a short overland portage, probably accomplished in about six hours, took one across the neck of the Cape from a few miles up the Scusset River, entered from Cape Cod Bay, and thus avoided the hazards of sea passage around the Cape.

Just at this time the Pilgrims took advantage of a new contact. Responding to earlier Dutch offers to trade for beaver, Governor Bradford invited Isaack de Rasieres, the chief merchant in New Amsterdam, to pay a visit. The portly burgher arrived at the Aptucxet post in October 1627 and came ashore "accompanied with a noise of trumpeters." Finding the journey overland to Plymouth too far to walk, he requested that a small boat be sent for him, visited the little town, and in due course wrote a description of it. The intercourse thus opened with the Dutch plantation at the mouth of the Hudson lasted several years. It not only offered the

Pilgrims desirable goods, such as sugar, linen cloth, and other stuffs, but in the long run greatly enhanced the colony's opportunities for Indian trade by selling them a quantity of wampum. This valuable native shell money, made by the Narragansetts, now promoted gainful dealings with the Abnakis of the Kennebec country and other tribes. De Rasieres felt it necessary to justify his selling the Pilgrims the first fifty fathom of sewan (wampum) by saying that he hoped to keep them from seeking it themselves at its source of manufacture and so discovering the profitable fur trade inland. He must have meant by this the trade with the Iroquois the Dutch had tapped through their control of the Hudson River, or that of the upper Connecticut Valley. **[38]**

Plymouth obtains a new patent to protect its trading rights

The rival shipmasters and settlers now ranging along the rocky coves and inlets of the Maine coast alarmed Plymouth lest they take control of the mouth of the Kennebec River. Since the autumn of 1625, most of the beaver collected had been furnished by the Abnaki Indians of this region. To secure this area and to define the boundaries of the colony, which had been unspecified in the Peirce patent, Isaac Allerton was directed to seek a new patent from the Council for New England. Some money was laid out for this purpose in his accounts with Sherley in 1628. The first grant he obtained proved to be so "strait and ill bounded," however, that he had to apply for its enlargement. Sherley reported that Allerton was "so turmoiled about it" that he would not have undertaken such trouble, even for a thousand pounds.

The fruit of these efforts was a patent the Council issued in 1630, signed by the Earl of Warwick. It gave Plymouth not only its first exact boundaries, but a strip of land along the Kennebec, with control of fifteen miles on either side of the river, running up the river as far as the site of Cushenoc or present-day Augusta, Maine. This document, in the name of William Bradford and his associates, the first of their grants reflecting the complete shift in ownership from London to the New World, provided the basis for the colony's land rights. At the same time Allerton did not succeed in getting past the seals a charter from the King, such as Massachusetts Bay had. He was criticized for this, somewhat unjustly, on the grounds that he failed because he and Sherley included among its terms some special customs privileges. Yet several charters, notably that of Massachusetts Bay, carried privileges similar to those Allerton requested, so it is more likely that a lack of funds and influence at court blocked passage. Allerton had apparently influenced Sherley to persuade Bradford that this charter could be secured only if he was allowed to go back to England. In fact, nothing more came of it, although £500 was reported to have been spent on the patent. **[39]**

Plymouth's business agent is dismissed for a "conflict of interest"

Until this time everyone had relied on Allerton; now the "Undertakers" began to look on their business agent with disfavor. His previous long record of helpfulness had caused them to disregard the grumblings of the new settlers from Leyden, who were dissatisfied with his treatment of them. Allerton had belonged to the original Leyden congregation and had helped advise Carver and Cushman about preparations for the voyage to America, had signed the Mayflower Compact, and had assisted Governor Bradford after Carver's death. As a member of the governing circle and a trusted official, he completed negotiation of the dissolution of the merchant adventurers for New Plymouth during trips to London in 1626–27. Quite naturally, Sherley's praise of him as an "honest and discreet agent" bolstered the colony's belief in his "good and faithful service."

While this enterprising man began his mission without deliberately dishonest intent, he expected successfully to combine with it the pursuit of his own private interests. He soon joined Sherley in a private arrangement, for in 1628 the London man referred to an "account betwixt you and me," which was separate from Allerton's purchases for Plymouth. There it was known and accepted that he brought over some goods "upon his own particular, and sold them for his own ... benefit." His frequent journeys to England and the intimate knowledge he had of the needs of New England obviously gave him special opportunities. One of these was to buy provisions for the settlers of Massachusetts Bay, a contract perhaps dating from a visit he made aboard the ship carrying John Winthrop to New England in 1630. Emmanuel Downing and John Humfrey, two leading supporters in London of the Bay colony, thought highly of his advice that they move this plantation to the Hudson River. Allerton's relation with the Bay leaders outlasted those with the Pilgrims. **[40]**

Plymouth's agent nonetheless revealed an indifference to her wishes when he brought back from England the very same Thomas Morton whom she had expelled. It was an insult to shelter this man right on the main street and even to employ him for a short time as a business secretary. Then, too, while buying a much bigger quantity of goods to be sold to the settlers than instructed, Allerton neglected to secure proper supplies of trading goods. Sherley had pressured him into exceeding the small quotas ordered by the

"Undertakers," he said in his defense. Sherley's letters did stress, of course, the need to turn over as large an amount as possible during the relatively short duration of the partnership's monopoly of trade, arguing that a large outlay was required to make a good profit in so short a time. "... we must follow it roundly and to purpose, for if we piddle out the time in our trade, others will step in and nose us...." Bradford and the others, understandably, were much more anxious to pay off the debts already owed than to overextend themselves just to make a profit. **[41]**

Such disagreements between Allerton and Sherley on the one hand, and Bradford, Winslow, and others at Plymouth, multiplied as the result of a new Maine venture, devised in 1629, which rivaled the Kennebec. Sherley and three other Londoners sent Edward Ashley, a keen trader but "a profane young man" by Pilgrim standards, to found a rival post at Pentagoet, near the Penobscot River. Allerton had refused to commit the Plymouth partners to the scheme without their consent, but on the basis of later correspondence Bradford decided that he had been an instigator of the plan. Since they had to send Ashley supplies, the Pilgrims had little choice anyway but to come in, if they wished to have some control of this potential competitor. Ashley soon was better supplied with trading goods than Plymouth, which, indeed, had to buy from Allerton himself, in return for part of their beaver taken at reduced prices. Without their knowledge, their versatile agent next borrowed money on their account at Bristol, at 50% interest, ostensibly so that goods might be shipped early with the fishing fleet headed for New England waters in the spring of the year.

Meanwhile, Winslow had conceived a plan to send a fishing ship laden with trading goods from the West Country in England directly to Maine, where a cargo of salt purchased the season before would await the ship's arrival. In fact, the vessel thus hired, the *Friendship,* was badly delayed by "foul weather" so that Allerton reached Maine, traveling on the *White Angel*, only just before Timothy Hatherley, one of the London associates, finally reached Boston in the *Friendship*. The latter revealed that most of the goods he carried were not for Plymouth at all, but for Massachusetts. Plymouth's mounting annoyance and mistrust of Allerton reached its pinnacle with the disturbing revelation that the English partners had bought outright the *White Angel*, not merely hired her, as was customary. The "Undertakers" suddenly were confronted by fresh, crushing debts, for each English partner had contributed two or three times as large an investment as before. Meanwhile, with a subtle note of mistrust of Plymouth's dealings with them, the latter had designated Hatherley as a confidential agent to be informed of "the state and account of all the business." **[42]**

Thus commenced a new and tedious financial wrangle between Plymouth and London. The former felt that the necessary control of their own business and obligations ceased when the English members could "run into such great things, and charge of shipping and new projects in their own heads, not only without but against all order and advice...." Confronted by their objections, Allerton undertook to convince them that they need not have the *White Angel* on the general account, if they did not wish to. Years later, in 1639, he testified that he had bought her at Bristol in 1631 only for the inner group comprising himself, Sherley, Andrews, and Beauchamp, and even Hatherley, whereas the *Friendship* was hired for all the partners of Plymouth. London contradicted this, saying that the ship would not have been purchased at all, if it hadn't been for the interests of Plymouth.

The disagreement over the *White Angel* and the *Friendship* plagued the partnership for some time to come, but the leaders on both sides of the Atlantic now concurred in the dismissal of Allerton as agent. Hatherley's tour of inspection of the "down east" trading posts before his return to London demonstrated to him that "Allerton played his own game and ran a course not only to the great wrong and detriment of the Plantation who employed and trusted him, but abused them ... in possessing them [in England] with prejudice against the Plantation ... that they would never be able to repay their moneys...." Winslow, one of the most enterprising traders among the "Undertakers," had journeyed to London earlier in 1631 and succeeded the discredited agent.

Should Allerton flatly be called a cheat? Unable to "be brief in so tedious and intricate a business," Bradford himself struggled not to impute to Allerton thoroughly dishonest motives. The Governor even admitted that the agent's commission to act in Plymouth's behalf had given him a certain freedom of action. That Allerton had been led aside from the main desires of the Plantation by "his own gains and private ends," we conclude from his managing to invest £400 under Sherley's name in the brewhouse belonging to one of the former London adventurers, William Collier. Bradford became convinced that the agent had inspired both the schemes of Ashley's rival trade and the purchase of the *White Angel*, persuading his London friends that the Kennebec trade alone was insufficient to pay them.

The partnership's general account thus became simply a convenient place for Allerton to unload losses, with records "so large and intricate, as they could not well understand them, much less examine and correct them without a great deal of time and help...." His lists of all sorts of expenses took advantage of the Pilgrims' weakness with accounts: "£30 given at a clap, and £50 spent in a journey.... Yea, he screwed up his poor old father-in-law's [Elder Brewster] account to above £200 and brought it upon the general account ... because he knew they would never let it lie on the old man...." Puzzled, Bradford admitted that he did not know "how it came to pass, or what mystery was in it," that Allerton even was able to present a list of all "disbursements," though it was Sherley who made them during his own absence. In the final calculations a sizable discrepancy (£2300) arose. Whereas the agent claimed the partners owed him £300, the latter represented his debt to them as £2000.

When Sherley wrote that "if their business had been better managed they might have been the richest plantation of any English at that time," he could blame the financial incompetence of the "Undertakers" at Plymouth as well as Allerton's deficiencies. Their initial trust in the honesty of others, however praiseworthy, was no match for the shrewdness of the businessmen who soon were to make Boston and the Bay colony the center of trade in New England. Consider how they accepted their associate Hatherley's unauthorized "honest word" that they would be discharged from the *Friendship*'s account, thus permitting Allerton and him to collect all its returns, even though they paid the Pilgrims only £200. Then, after Hatherley's London partners repudiated this discharge, the Pilgrims were billed for losses, but with no countervailing credits. "... they were ... now taught how to deal in the world, especially with merchants, in such cases," Bradford sadly noted in comment, but the lesson unfortunately did not improve their keeping of accounts. **[43]**

Without a single surviving letter of Allerton's, stating his point of view about the Pilgrims, it is difficult to judge his career. We know that as a busy merchant and projector he continued to shuttle back and forth across the Atlantic and up and down the American coast from northern Maine to New Amsterdam. His own ventures in the *White Angel*, which he hired and later bought from Sherley, turned out badly, but the fault of placing part of its debts on Plymouth's account seems to have been Sherley's. Allerton set up a rival post at Machias, Maine, "to run into every hole and into the river of the Kennebec to glean away the trade ... there"; after its capture by the French, his pinnace traded in the Penobscot region. During a season of fishing at Marblehead for Matthew Cradock, a London promoter of the Massachusetts Bay Company, Allerton nevertheless continued to be named an assistant of the Plymouth colony and was a freeman there as late as 1637. In 1633 he was the richest man in Plymouth; he lent large sums of money to other settlers, including his sister's husband. Merchants of Massachusetts and New Netherland did not distrust him, even though Winslow wrote from England in 1637 to warn Governor Winthrop of Massachusetts that Allerton was too friendly with "our common adversaries," those who were thinking of securing a royal commission to govern all of New England. He wrote: "... the truth is he loveth neither you nor us."

The former agent was, in fact, primarily a businessman, without strong religious or sentimental ties. He certainly "abused" the trust of his old comrades by saddling them with such heavy debts, but his acts seem unscrupulous rather than calculated dishonesty. He took risks which, if they turned out badly, hurt other people. In short, this maker of "fair propositions and large promises" was led into temptation by dreams of wealth; in this he was like many another promoter. Ultimately, his bad judgment and ill luck brought him losses, and he died insolvent in New Haven in 1659. **[44]**

The colony and its London partners dispute over their accounts

The stresses between the "Undertakers" and the London partners were not relieved simply by Allerton's dismissal. A decade of acrimonious exchange of letters followed from 1631 to 1641. It was not easy for the Londoners to balance off Allerton's debts, along with new expenses, against the receipt of furs shipped from Plymouth. They were determined to hold out until a settlement profitable to them was reached. Throughout this quarrel Bradford's *History* has to be our guide for the most part, for only one fragment of reckoning between Sherley and Allerton has been found. Undoubtedly, when the great governor wrote his narrative he was trying to rehabilitate the Pilgrims' financial reputation and counter the rumors in London and Boston mercantile circles that they were in default. In his chapters on finance he is repetitious, sometimes confusing, and yet omits certain business details. His judgment was charitable, however, and by recording Sherley's letters he preserved at least some of London's side of the controversy.

The first dispute arose from Edward Winslow's unwillingness to accept the *White Angel*'s losses on the "Undertakers'" account. Sherley was displeased and warned that this "unreasonable refusal" might "hasten that fire which is a kindling too fast already...." Plymouth nonetheless declined to take on all the debts which appeared in Sherley's accounting of 1631. It was found that in arriving at a total of £4770, in addition to £1000 unpaid of the purchase money, he had charged twice and even three times for certain items. £600 of this amount even Allerton could not identify.

The London partners' dissatisfaction with the records kept in Plymouth led Sherley to insist on the appointment of Josiah Winslow, younger brother of Edward, as their accountant. The Pilgrims remarked crustily "that if they were well dealt with and had their goods well sent over, they could keep their accounts ... themselves." Certainly, the new accountant, with his hopeless inaccuracy and carelessness, did little to mend matters. In fact, he "did wholly fail them, and could never give them any account; but trusting to his memory and loose papers, let things run into such confusion that neither he, nor any with him, could bring things to rights." Ultimately, they lost several hundreds of pounds in this way for goods trusted out without any record clear enough to call in the payments. Also, goods arrived from England without prices or invoices.

Meanwhile, several circumstances fed Plymouth's dissatisfaction with James Sherley, including his continuing to do business with Allerton. After selling the latter the controversial ship, Sherley nevertheless could write with unctious fervor, "Oh the grief and trouble that man, Mr. Allerton, hath brought upon you and us! I cannot forget it, and to think on it draws many a sigh from my heart and tears from my eyes." Yet he rescued Allerton from trouble with his ship, sent Plymouth's supply on board it in 1632, and allowed him easy terms. It was hard to reconcile Sherley's depressing complaints about his own heavy debts with this extension of credit to Allerton and participation in other ventures, such as sending Captain William Peirce to Massachusetts Bay. Unfortunately, Peirce's ship met disaster on her way home in 1632, so the beaver that Plymouth had entrusted to her, along with some of their accounts, was "swallowd up in the sea."

By 1636 Bradford reckoned that Plymouth had sent to England about 12,530 pounds of beaver estimated to be worth more than £10,000, with 1,156 otter skins to pay the freight charges. Because of Winslow's shaky accounts, they could only estimate the receipts of English goods. They thought these cost about £2000, and even if the debt of £4770 was increased, they could not understand why the fur receipts would not have more than paid it off. One explanation probably is that Sherley was unable to sell all of the beaver at the high prices they had counted on. During the plague year of 1636 he complained that prices dropped to 8s. a pound. Also, Sherley was unable to determine just how many skins belonged to the "Undertakers'" account, and how many Winslow had bought from settlers who had no part in the "Undertakers'" scheme. **[45]**

The London partners quarrel among themselves

To the problem of extricating the Plymouth venture from its financial straits a new one was now added. A quarrel had broken out among the English partners themselves, James Sherley, John Beauchamp, and Richard Andrews. These men had shared in the debts incurred after 1626 to keep Plymouth supplied. The Pilgrims had expected all three to profit from the large quantities of furs shipped after 1631. Instead, in 1640 Beauchamp and Andrews revealed a rift with Sherley of several years standing. They complained in court that they had not received a fair share of the returns on their investment and tried to force a full accounting of Sherley's transactions with Plymouth. This suit, with its contradictory sets of figures, exposed the nature of their association.

In the joint adventure to trade with the Governor and the rest of the Plymouth "Undertakers," each of the three Londoners had promised to put £1100 into stock. Richard Andrews paid in £1136, John Beauchamp £1127, and, they claimed, James Sherley pretended to put in £1190 (a total of about £3500). To meet pressing debts about 1636 Beauchamp contributed £500 more. It was expected that Sherley, acting as sole factor, would dispose of returns from the plantation, report occasionally to them, and distribute any profits. In a few years, they asserted, he handled beaver and otter worth from £12,000 to £13,000 but ignored their requests to show his accounts; thus they had no way of checking whether he had used some of the profits for his own business. He had exhibited "a covetous disposition to gain ... [their dues] himself ..." and to their "loving" pleas replied violently that he would rot and die before giving an account. They suspected him of withdrawing his own stock and profits.

How did Sherley answer these charges? First, he denied that Andrews was a party to the suit, since before going abroad, he had told Sherley of Beauchamp's plan to sue and refused to join in it. Not he, but Allerton, had been the "Undertakers'" agent, accredited to buy and sell; he acted only in Allerton's absence, although permitting his warehouse in London to be used for Plymouth's goods. In 1632 he had given Edward Winslow copies of all his receipts and payments. Since the chief function of all three London merchants had consisted of making good Allerton's demands for credit for Plymouth, they had laid out sizable sums of money, urged on by hope of preventing loss of what they had already invested. Sherley alone found himself "out of purse" some £1866 in March 1631/32. If he was able to collect £675 owed to Plymouth, this still left him with £1190 tied up in their enterprise. The debts of the London men, on Plymouth's behalf, ran up to £5900 in 1631, but Sherley had been paying these off slowly, as the planters' returns trickled in. Indeed, had it not been for his own "deep engagements" and his partners' "earnest request," Sherley protested, he would have given up the business long before. He was not obliged to give a detailed accounting to his copartners, but only to the Plymouth associates. Actually, it was up to the latter to produce an exact accounting to the three London men, not the other way about. Sherley was anxious to reconcile his accounts with them and was willing to meet their agent even in France or Holland; until then, he could not even "book" (enter) the items for which he had loose records.

Sherley insisted that he had sold no furs for his own profit, but had informed Beauchamp and Andrews when he disposed of any. In a final balance of all records he was sure that Plymouth would still owe him money, not he owe his copartners, for the latter had adventured absolutely nothing since 1631. He, not they, had carried the burden in London in the "sickly" years of 1635 and 1636. With this defense, Bradford says, Beauchamp and Andrews failed to win the suit,_**[46]**_ and indeed, Sherley's letters confirm that his credit was sorely taxed in the 1630s.

Through arbiters, Plymouth and London reach a financial settlement

While this dispute was in progress, however, the Pilgrims were so perplexed about its rights that they were persuaded to send 1,325 pounds of beaver directly to the other two partners, hoping to satisfy their claims that Sherley had paid them nothing. After selling it, Beauchamp chalked off £400 of their debt, but Andrews, through mismanagement, sold his at a loss and in 1642 still claimed between £500 and £600. He finally agreed to accept payment in cattle to Governor John Winthrop of Massachusetts Bay and designated the "godly poor men" and "poor ministers" of that colony as the beneficiaries of Plymouth's debt. In addition, Andrews and Beauchamp received land in Scituate, one of several flourishing daughter towns now settled in Plymouth._**[47]**_

Meanwhile the business with Sherley was wound up at last. Trade with him had already broken off because of distrust of his repeated delays in accounting to his London partners. For fear of legal reprisals from any of these, it was decided not to risk sending another agent to London but to have some "gentlemen and merchants in the Bay" hear the dispute. Even "though it should cost them all they had in the world," the "Undertakers" promised to accept their award. This decision was prompted by two considerations. First, they feared that the price of cattle, by now a greater source of income than furs, might drop and change their circumstances. Also, the colony's founders, surviving into old age, wished to clear up their affairs before death overtook them. Sherley himself believed that lawyers would be "the most gainers" from legal action, and therefore selected John Atwood and William Collier, recent merchant arrivals in Plymouth from London, to draw up a composition. Another participant in the settlement was Edmund Freeman, Beauchamp's brother-in-law, and now the leading citizen of Sandwich. After laborious days of investigation of accounts, they estimated everything left in Plymouth of the old stock, housing, boats, the bark and goods for the Indian trade, and "all debts, as well those that were desperate, as others more hopeful," at £1400.

By October 15, 1641, Atwood, Bradford, and Edward Winslow had come to terms ending the partnership. The agreement of 1627 was reacknowledged, but Plymouth, while admitting confusion in Josiah Winslow's bookkeeping, again repudiated the debts of the *White Angel* and the *Friendship*. A full discharge from the obligations of the beaver trade, the charges of the two ships, and the £1800 purchase money agreed on in 1627 was promised by Atwood in behalf of the London associates. Bradford and his partners for their part guaranteed payment to them of £1400. £110 of this had already been paid to Winthrop for Andrews' account, and eighty pounds of beaver to Atwood. The rest was to be discharged in appropriate commodities, at the rate of £200 per year.

1645 – Plymouth's debts "hopeful and desperate" at last are discharged

To execute this agreement across the distance of the broad Atlantic took some time. Recognizing the justness of the "Undertakers'" final account but calling the venture "uncomfortable and unprofitable to all," James Sherley signed the release in June 1642. In the bargaining, the Reverend Hugh Peter, Thomas Weld, and William Hibbins, in England as agents of Massachusetts, put forth Atwood's terms. At the same time they succeeded in persuading the London partners to surrender for charitable purposes in New England the £1200 debt. Three quarters, or £900, was set apart for Massachusetts, while Plymouth was to receive only £300.

A letter of Richard Andrews about this time fortunately permits us to break away from the divergent points of view set forth in Bradford's narrative and Sherley's letters. In many ways Andrews was the most straightforward of the London partners and the most generous. While forgiving the interest due on his own account, he charged that Sherley and Beauchamp had "wronged [the business] many £100 both in principal and interest" and knowingly presented unfair accounts. This remark suggests one solution to the problem as to why the seemingly excessive charges on the Pilgrims mounted year after year in spite of their returns. Hinting that Sherley had manipulated some private losses so as to place them on the general account, Andrews perhaps did not recognize the rapidity with which the debts accumulated because of the high rates of interest on them. The fact is that colonial ventures were considered such poor financial risks that their debts tended to multiply faster than they could be paid off. This explanation of their financial plight is probably closer to the truth than that the Londoners deliberately perpetrated a "manifest fraud" upon the plantation. It was Andrews also who echoed the complaint common to all the London merchants engaged in colonial enterprise. He wrote in 1645 that the conduct of the "Undertakers" did not become "fair dealing men who make not so much profession to walk according to the rule of the gospel as they.... I hope that seven years time is long enough to keep my money before they return the principal...."

John Beauchamp, unlike the more generous Andrews, continued to insist on collecting his debt even though it could never be proved. To settle this claim, Bradford and his partners in 1645 turned over to his attorney houses and lands in Plymouth, Rehoboth, and Marshfield worth £291. **[48]**

It is to Plymouth's credit that all these obligations were met in the 1640s, because the colony was no longer as prosperous as in the preceding decade. Its wealth had come to consist increasingly of cattle, so that the price collapse which took place when the influx of new settlers into the Bay ceased, came suddenly and with severe effect. Cattle came to be worth perhaps 25% of its former value. Even the wealthier colony of Massachusetts discovered that it could no longer secure credit in England. The Pilgrims nevertheless continued to develop their modest resources in animal stock and land. A new land arrangement reflected the ending of the old debts. Governor Bradford, who had held title to the patent since 1630, along with the "old comers" or "purchasers," turned over the grant to the whole body of freemen of Plymouth, retaining for himself only three reserved tracts as his reward for carrying the responsibility for repayment.

As to Plymouth's fur trade, the complaint John Winthrop had once voiced that the colony had "engrossed all the chief places of trade" in New England was no longer true. The "Old Colony" had been edged out of the Connecticut River and Narragansett trade, some of its Maine posts had been attacked by the French, and rival settlers and competitors had made the rest less profitable. At Aptucxet commerce with the Dutch kept on for a time, and on the Kennebec there remained an echo of the busy activity of the 1630s. A small group farmed the Indian trade there so that at his death in 1657 Bradford's stock of trading goods and debts due from it was worth £256. Within a few years, however, all trading goods were brought home and the Kennebec tract sold. **[49]**

Thus ended the history of Plymouth Colony as a business venture. Even after careful study of all the details we know, it is hard to interpret and correctly assess whether the London capitalists or the colony can really be blamed for the contradictory financial muddle. In their somewhat uneasy alliance, the Londoners with spare funds and the group of obscure artisans and small farmers, mostly dissenters from the established church, no doubt emphasized different goals. Most of the merchants, while Puritan in religious sympathies, nevertheless anticipated profits. This appeared to them fitting, since they risked great loss in so untried a speculation. Then, after Plymouth was settled and valuable returns established, the Londoners held an advantage to the end, for they were always in a creditor position as they continued to supply essential goods at high prices and rates of interest. The colonists' payment was slow, interrupted by many misfortunes and contingencies, but eventually it was made. Although the investors in the original company lost most of their money, the businessmen who stayed with the enterprise, such as Sherley, seem to have increased their capital.

The Pilgrims, too, achieved success, for they had built the essentials of a free and self-sustaining community. If they were never wealthy in their new environment, the leaders of Plymouth, developing business experience and judgment, by 1645 enjoyed modest prosperity. They had paid off the expenses of shipping over their fellow exiles from Leyden and bought the livestock and equipment needed as the foundation for settlement. Ignorance, desertion by their first backers, cruel losses at sea, their agent's misdeeds, all had been overcome. They were now rid of the burdens inherent in the London merchants' sponsorship of the colony. Their debts, both "hopeful and 68desperate," lay behind.

Notes

[1] William Bradford, *Of Plymouth Plantation*, ed. Samuel E. Morison (New York, 1952), 16–17, 24, 27, 33, 49. Quotations will ordinarily be from this modernized version of Governor Bradford's history. Quotations from other sources have been modernized. Henry Martyn Dexter, *The England and Holland of the Pilgrims* (Boston, 1905), App. 601–641, for list of occupations; Roland G. Usher, *The Pilgrims and Their History* (New York, 1918), 35–40, on the economic and religious motives for removal.

[2] John Smith, *Description of New England* (1616), is in Smith, *Works*, ed. Edward Arber (Westminster, 1895), ii; for Brewster's copy, see "Plymouth Colony, Wills and Inventories," 1641–1649 (typescript, Pilgrim Hall, Plymouth, Mass.), 49; Bradford, *Of Plymouth Plantation*, ed. Morison, 28–29; Smith's comment on the Pilgrims, Bradford, *History of Plymouth Plantation*, ed. W. C. Ford, 2 vols. (Boston, 1912), i, 192n. Edward Winslow, *Hypocrisie Unmasked* (1646), told the story about consulting God's will, cited *ibid.*, 66n.

[3] Bradford, *History*, ed. Ford, i, 70n., 77n. Winslow reported the King's conversation long after Plymouth's settlement in *Hypocrisie Unmasked*, cited in Bradford, *Of Plymouth Plantation*, ed. Morison, 30n. It sounds a bit overdrawn. William Brewster, a former tenant of the Sandys family, may have introduced his associates to Sir Edwin Sandys.

[4] Charles M. Andrews, *The Colonial Period of American History* (New Haven, 1934), i, 254–255, describes the system of private plantations. Bradford, *Of Plymouth Plantation*, ed. Morison, 35, 37, identifying the offer of support by Thomas Weston; the 1619 patent in Susan M. Kingsbury, ed., *The Records of the Virginia Company* (Washington, 1906), i, 221, 228; Edward Arber, ed., *Story of the Pilgrim Fathers* (London, 1897), ch. xxv, on Brewster; Bradford, *Of Plymouth Plantation*, ed. Morison, 356–357, for Cushman's report on Blackwell.

[5] On the Dutch offer, Bradford, *History*, ed. Ford, i, 99n. See *Mass. Hist. Soc. Proc.*, liv, 166, 168, 177, and Astrid Friis, *Alderman Cockayne's Project and the Cloth Trade* (Copenhagen and London, 1927), 370, for Weston as an ironmonger and "interloper." The lawsuit against Weston filed in the Court of Exchequer by Pickering's executors, John Fowler, James Sherley, and Richard Andrews, appears to confirm a streak of dishonesty in Weston. The original depositions and award include interesting details about some of the Plymouth partners and their associates, *Mass. Hist. Soc. Proc.*, liv (1922), 165–178 (summaries); P.R.O., E. 134, 22 James i, Mich. 22; Mich. 59; Hilary 22/8. The award, E. 178/5451, was kindly transcribed for me by Prof. Norma Adams. "Governor Bradford's Letter Book," i *Mass. Hist. Soc. Colls.*, iii (1794), 27, on Weston's debts to partners.

[6] John Smith, *A Description of New England* (1616), is a plea for fishing and plantation; also Smith's letter to Sir Francis Bacon, 1618, transcript in Bancroft Mss., New England (New York Public Library), i, 19–23.

[7] Bradford, *Of Plymouth Plantation*, ed. Morison, 49–50, 43, 42, 44, 50, 55.

[8] £1200 Cushman reported raised by June 1620 still left them £300 or £400. Bradford, *Of Plymouth Plantation*, ed. Morison, 45–46, 55, 56; 104n., quoting John Smith, *Generall Historie ...* (1626); 49, 50, 57, on sale of supplies; 60, on landfall. Nathaniel Morton, *New England's Memoriall* (1669), (Boston, 1903), 30, on Carver.

[9] Bradford, *Of Plymouth Plantation*, ed. Morison, 75n.; Bradford, *History*, ed. Ford, i, 234n., 246f. for the text and a photograph of the original indenture now on exhibit in Pilgrim Hall; Frances Rose-Troup, *Massachusetts Bay Company and its Predecessors* (New York, 1930), 3–4, explains the difference between an indenture and a patent.

[10] Bradford, *Of Plymouth Plantation*, ed. Morison, 93, Weston's letter; Henry Martyn Dexter, ed., *Mourt's Relation or Journal of the Plantation at Plymouth* (Boston, 1865).

[11] Bradford, *Of Plymouth Plantation*, ed. Morison, 95; Cushman's discourse, printed as *A Sermon Preached at Plimoth in New England* ... (London, 1622), is reprinted in part in Alexander Young, *Chronicles of the Pilgrim Fathers* (2d ed., Boston, 1844), 255–268.

[12] See note 5 above; Bradford, *Of Plymouth Plantation*, ed. Morison, 100–103, 104, 105, 107, 119; Treasury warrant, Ms. Calendar of Cranfield Papers, 8680, Hist. Mss. Commission, P.R.O., London. Charles Francis Adams, *Three Episodes in Massachusetts History* (Boston, 1892) i, 45–104, is still the most readable account of Weston's colony at Wessagusset, although inaccurate in a few details.

[13] Dexter, *Mourt's Relation*, xxxv-xxxviii; Bradford, *Of Plymouth Plantation*, ed. Morison, 124–125; *New Eng. Hist. Gen. Reg.*, lxvii, 147–153; P.R.O., C2/P44/43, Peirce's suit. Andrews, *Col. Per. Amer. Hist.*, i, 281–282 and 282n., takes Bradford to task for "pretty deliberate misrepresentation" of the Peirce matter. The search in English records for information on Peirce proved unusually difficult, because of the commonness of his name. For example, two John Peirces were admitted to the Clothworkers' Company, one in 1597, the other in 1612 (letter to author from Mr. J. E. Coombes, Clerk, Clothworkers' Company, Aug. 9, 1961). Mr. Coombes' report of scanty records for the period precluded further search. A Mr. John Peirce sold John Winthrop provisions, *Winthrop Papers* (Boston, 1931–47), iii, 3, 4, 5.

[14] The leaders of the adventurers named by Peirce in his Chancery suit were James Sherley, John Pocock, Christopher Coulson, William Collier, John Thornell, and George [Robert] Keane, *New Eng. Hist. Gen. Reg.*, lxvii, 149. Usher, *The Pilgrims and Their History*, 147–148, and John A. Goodwin, *The Pilgrim Republic* (Boston, 1888), 252–254, sum up the misadventures of the *Little James*. The original evidence is in Bradford, *History*, ed. Ford, i, 341–346, 350–351, 403–405, 433–435. Additional details are in the Admiralty suit of two crew members, Stephens and Fell, *Mass. Hist. Soc. Proc.*, lxi, 148–151; H. C. A., Instance and Prize Court, Libel Files, Bundle 82, no. 124 (Library of Congress transcript). An effort to locate this document in the Public Record Office under this reference was unsuccessful.

[15] For the transcript of Altham's letters to his brother, Sir Edward Altham, Sept. 1623, Mar. 1623/24, June 10, 1625, I am indebted to Dr. Sydney V. James's "Three Visitors to Early Plymouth," a typescript in the possession of Plimoth Plantation. The original letters belonged to Dr. Otto Fisher of Detroit, Michigan, who gave permission for use of quotations. James, "Three Visitors," 36, 42, 46, 50. Altham invested some of his friends'

money in the common stock and suggested that if he came back on a fishing voyage, he could use £400 or £500 of their ventures, *ibid.*, 62, 66.

[16] William Bradford and Isaac Allerton to the adventurers, Sept. 1623, *Amer. Hist. Rev.*, viii, 297; John W. Thornton, *The Landing at Cape Anne* (Boston, 1854); Goodwin, *Pilgrim Republic*, 255; Bradford, *History*, ed. Ford, i, 377–379, 407–410, for the patent.

[17] Bradford, *Of Plymouth Plantation*, ed. Morison, 120–121, 132, 144–145, 187; Edward Winslow, *Good Newes from New England* (1624) in Young, *Chronicles of the Pilgrims*, 346–347; Bradford, *History*, ed. Ford, i, 300n.

[18] For further light on these factions, see James, "Three Visitors," 104ff., letter of June 10, 1625.

[19] *Ibid.*, 70, 72; Bradford, *Of Plymouth Plantation*, ed. Morison, 170; Bradford, "Letter Book," 28, 34, 29, 32.

[20] The most complete list of investors in Plymouth is that of the signers of the composition of 1626, *ibid.*, 48. To these should be added Christopher Coulson, William Greene, John Peirce, Edward Pickering, and Thomas Weston. The Plymouth leaders accepted in 1627 the terms the merchants had signed in November 1626. Thus it is correct to refer to 1627 as the date of the final business settlement with the original company.

[21] W. R. Scott, *The Constitution and Finance of English ... Joint-Stock Companies* (London, 1910), ii, 310–311, calculated the share capital as £5600. Sherley spent the best part of £5000 in two years as treasurer. This probably did not include the period when Weston was in charge, Bradford, "Letter Book," 49. On debts of £1400, see *ibid.*, 32.

[22] Smith is quoted in Bradford, *History*, ed. Ford, i, 104n. Andrews observed that even though the names of a number of the adventurers were known, "of only a few can any further information be obtained," *Col. Per. Amer. Hist.*, i, 287n. The research on which the following paragraphs are based is probably the most sustained effort so far to find out more. The late Col. Charles E. Banks was interested chiefly in tracing the emigrants to Plymouth; see *Mass. Hist. Soc. Proc.*, lxi, 55–63, "William Bradford and the Pilgrim Quarter in London."

For Sir Thomas Andrews, see Valerie Pearl, *London and the Outbreak of the Puritan Revolution* (Oxford, 1961), 309–311, 208, 240, 242. This work is invaluable for its mass of biographical detail about London merchants, interpretation of London's role, and bibliography. J. C. Whitebrook, "Sir Thomas Andrewes, Lord Mayor and Regicide, and his Relatives," *Trans. Congregational Hist. Soc.*, xiii (1938–39), 151–165, informs us that Damaris

Andrews, daughter of Thomas, married the son of Matthew Cradock, first governor of the Massachusetts Bay Company. The Richard Andrews connected with Plymouth and Massachusetts Bay, appears to be the brother of Thomas, *ibid.*, 159. For Thomas's official career, see C. H. Firth and R. S. Rait, eds., *Acts and Ordinances of the Interregnum, 1642–60* (London, 1911), 2 vols., *passim*, esp. i, 1150, 1255; ii, 365, 595, 647, 917; A. B. Beaven, *The Aldermen of London* (London, 1908), ii, 66. As an active member of the directorate of the East India Company, he was expert on shipping and the sale of Company wares; see E. B. Sainsbury, ed., *Cal. Court Mins. E. I. Co., 1635–1676* (Oxford, 1907–35), iii, xi, xvi, xxii-xxiii, 218, 222, 128, 224, 267; v, xxxii, 333. Among summaries of Independency in the Civil Wars, see J. R. Tanner, *English Constitutional Conflicts of the 17th Century* (Cambridge, repr. 1947), 128; Pearl, *London and the Outbreak*, 6, who reminds us of the distinction between religious Independents and "political independents." The complex situation in England is not easy to summarize.

[23] This list has formerly been given as six, Bradford, *Of Plymouth Plantation*, ed. Morison, 185n., and slightly different in Bradford, *History*, ed. Ford, ii, 7n. I add Richard Andrews and Christopher Coulson and retain both Robert Keane and John White.

[24] For Richard Andrews' address, *Winthrop Papers*, ii, 306; Thomas Lechford, "Notebook," *Trans. Amer. Antiq. Soc.*, vii, 142; P.R.O., Exchequer, Depositions, E. 134, 22 James i, Mich. 59, on reverse of testimony by Francis Stubbs; Henry A. Harben, *A Dictionary of London* (London, 1918), 407. He may have resided in the ward of Cripplegate Within, where Richard Andrews, haberdasher, was one of the inhabitants most able to contribute to a Crown request for money, W. J. Harvey, ed., *List of Principal Inhabitants of London, 1640* (London, 1886), 14. For links to Massachusetts Bay, *Winthrop Papers*, ii, 306; *Recs. Mass. Bay*, i, 128; role as shipowner, *Cal. S. P. Domestic, 1628–29*, 440, and *1629–31*, 469; Netherlands trade, P.R.O., E. 134, 12 Charles i, Easter, 39, and Michaelmas, 23; *Winthrop Papers*, v, 4. Gifts to Massachusetts in *Winthrop's Journal*, ed. James K. Hosmer (New York, 1908), i, 128, and ii, 70, 222; and discussion in R. P. Stearns, "The Weld-Peter Mission to England," *Pubs. Col. Soc. Mass.*, xxxii, 199, and *The Strenuous Puritan: Hugh Peter* (Urbana, 1954), 162, erroneously calling Richard Andrews an alderman. *A.O.I., 1642–60*, i, 970, 1088, 1240, for his public service; P.R.O., S.P. 16/515/146; William Kellaway, *The New England Company, 1649–1776* (London, 1961), 66, for donations to a Puritan lectureship and to Indians; *idem*, "Collection for the

Indians of New England, 1649–1660," *Bull. John Rylands Library*, xxxix (1957), 458.

[25] Rose-Troup, *Mass. Bay Company and its Predecessors*, 138; *Recs. Mass. Bay*, i, 37c, 40; P.R.O., Close Rolls, C. 54/2635/ no. 8; Harvey, *Inhabitants of London*, 14; Pearl, *London and the Outbreak*, 169.

[26] *Winthrop's Journal*, ed. Hosmer, i, 15n., 30, 53; *Winthrop Papers*, ii, 309, 317, 339, and iii, 4, 5. Ownership of *Welcome*, S.P. 16/16/182. London addresses of Goffe in T. C. Dale, ed., *Inhabitants of London, 1638* (London, 1931), 112; "Return of Divided Houses ... London, 1637" (typescript, Guildhall Library), 115.

[27] E. N. Hartley, *Ironworks on the Saugus* (Norman, Okla., 1957), 69–70; Stearns, *The Strenuous Puritan*, 162, 166, 175, 180–181, 189; Bradford, *History*, ed. Ford, ii, 5n., and facsimile opp. 5. Hartley and Stearns disagree as to amount Pocock lent to Massachusetts Bay, but *Recs. Mass. Bay*, ii, 82, 262, and subsequent actions, appear to uphold the latter. Gift to St. Antholin's, S.P. 16/515/146; public service, *A.O.I. 1642–60*, i, 143, 233, 371, and ii, 1000.

[28] *Recs. Mass. Bay*, i, 60, 361, 386, 394, 395, 402, 367. Sharpe's later career has not been traced, but he is not especially prominent after arrival in Massachusetts.

[29] *Ibid.*, 60, 48, 53, 128. The ship's name probably was the *Eagle*, 400 tons. *Winthrop Papers*, ii, 215n., and iii, 3; *Winthrop's Journal*, ed. Hosmer, i, 44.

[30] Bernard Bailyn, "The *Apologia* of Robert Keayne," *Wm. and Mary Quarterly*, 3d ser., vii, 568–587. His will, *Report of the Record Commissioners of Boston*, x (Boston, 1886), 1–54; sermons attended in London, *Mass. Hist. Soc. Proc.*, 2d ser., l, 204–207. See *Recs. Mass. Bay*, i, 128; *Cal. S. P. Dom.*, 1627–28, 458; *New England Hist. Gen. Reg.*, lxvii, 247; Bradford, "Letter Book," 47; *Aspinwall Notarial Records 1644–51*, 92; *Winthrop Papers*, v, 351; Oliver A. Roberts, *History of the Military Company of the Massachusetts now called the Ancient and Honorable Artillery Company of Massachusetts 1637–1888* (Boston, 1895), i, 12, 20.

[31] Mary Freer Keeler, *The Long Parliament, 1640–41* (Philadelphia, 1954), 390; Frances Rose-Troup, *John White: the Patriarch of Dorchester ...* (New York, 1930), 56, 460, 163n., 73n.; *Winthrop Papers*, ii, 82n., 97; Andrews, *Col. Per. Amer. Hist.*, i, 345, citing Bradford, *History*, ed. Ford, i, 406. The correct reference is *ibid.*, 416. Isabel M. Calder, "A Seventeenth Century Attempt to Purify the Anglican Church," *Amer. Hist. Rev.*, liii, 761, 774n.; Pearl, *London*

and the Outbreak, 194–195. It is possible that the John White named as an owner of ships at Plymouth, Devon, is the lawyer, although it might also be John White of Dorchester, *Cal. S. P. Dom., 1628–29*, 301, 306, 440, 441; *ibid., 1629–31*, 154, 156.

[32] To identify John Beauchamp is particularly difficult. Ford has him as the son of Thomas Beauchamp of Cosgrave, Nottinghamshire. Using the same reference cited by him (*Visitation of London, 1633–35*, 59), I read it as Cosgrave, Northamptonshire. His marriage to Alice Freeman, whose brother, Edmund Freeman, acted as Beauchamp's attorney in Plymouth in 1641, seems to establish him as the right Beauchamp. See Bradford, *History*, ed. Ford, ii, 296n. Beaven makes John Beauchamp, Salter, Alderman for Billingsgate Ward in 1651, and gives as his will a reference to a John Beauchamp of the parish of St. Giles Cripplegate Without (Beaven, *Aldermen of London*, ii, 75; P.C.C. Hene [1668]), who left as heirs no wife or children, whereas the John Beauchamp connected with Plymouth had several sons and daughters. This will must be that of another man. In 1649 and after, a John Beauchamp of Surrey appeared in the same committees as James Sherley and Edward Winslow, such as those for collecting the army assessment or to sell goods from the estate of Charles i, *A.O.I., 1642–60*, ii, 44, 160, 310, 479, 676. See also Bradford, *Of Plymouth Plantation*, ed. Morison, 100, 198, 199, 386n.; Friis, *Alderman Cockayne's Project*, 110n.; P.R.O., Chancery, C. 3/431/12; *Cal. S. P. Dom.*, 1628–29, 285; Harvey, *Inhabitants of London, 1640*, 18; T. C. Dale, transcriber, "Citizens of London, 1641–43," (London, 1936; typescript, Guildhall Library).

[33] Bradford, "Letter Book," 34; Goldsmiths' Company, London, Apprentice Book, i, 1578–1645, 151; Wardens' Accounts and Court Minutes, vol. p, pt. 1 (1611–17), 76, 198; pt. 2 (1617–24), 189 and *passim*, 76, 77, 79; vol. q, pt. 1 (1624–29), 79; vol. r, pt. 2 (1631–34), 193, 195, 199, 200, 223, 224, 225; vol. t (1637–39), 185, 186, 189; vol. v (1639–42), 58, 62; vol. unlettered [w] (1642–45), 228, 237. Presumably because he was living in Clapham, James Sherley is not listed among those who paid poll money to the Commissioners. A duty of the prime warden, with his second and third wardens, was to have custody of the plate belonging to the City of London, *ibid.*, 238. In 1652 Sherley was appointed with other wardens to prepare an answer to a petition by the freemen of the Company to a committee of Parliament concerning their rights in choosing the wardens, Sir Walter S. Prideaux, *Memorials of the Goldsmiths' Company* ... (London, 1896), ii, 24.

Of the several James Sherleys who are contemporaries, I have concluded that the James Sherley, third son of Robert Sherley, originally of Wistonston, was the one involved with the Plymouth venture. The other James Sherleys in this family are (1) the eldest son of John Sherley of London, and (2) the elder son of James Sherley, son of Robert. See *Visitation of London, 1633–35*, ii, 235–236. It is difficult to determine whether the James Sherley, merchant, who owned houses in London in 1637 is the same, "Returns of Divided Houses in the City of London, 1637," 208. The one who appeared with Robert Sherley to turn over property to Robert's daughter, Sara, in 1632 is our man, P.R.O., C. 54/2950; see also *Registers of St. Vedast, Foster Lane* (Harl. Soc., 1902) 35, for birth of Sara in 1611.

"Foynes" or foins were originally fur of the weasel family, or more generally, furs.

[34] On Sherley's addresses, Marsden, *Amer. Hist. Rev.*, viii, 301; Plooij, *Pilgrim Fathers from a Dutch Point of View*, 100. Plooij says that London Bridge was his business address and Crooked Lane his "town house." I have been unable to verify it. Sir Ambrose Heal, *The London Goldsmiths, 1200–1800* (Cambridge, 1935), 242; Bradford, *Of Plymouth Plantation*, ed. Morison, 287; Acts of Administration, 1657 (Somerset House, London), fol. 242. Sherley's public appointments, *A.O.I.*, i, 730, and ii, 14, 310, 479, 676, 1082, 975; also William A. Shaw, *History of the English Church during the Civil Wars and under the Commonwealth* (London, 1900), ii, 434.

P.R.O., E. 134, 22 James i, Mich. 22; P.C.C. 86 Swann (1623); Bradford, "Letter Book," 68. The ships owned in part by Sherley were the *John and Mary* and the *Hector* of London, 220 tons and 250 tons respectively. Sherley refers to sending a letter in the *Mary and John*, very likely the same ship. A vessel of that name brought goods to Boston in 1633 and 1633/34, P.R.O., S.P. 16/17/83 and 16/17/117; *Winthrop Papers*, iii, 130, 149; Bradford, *Of Plymouth Plantation*, ed. Morison, 391; *Recs. Mass. Bay*, ii, 262. The *Lyon* sent to Boston in 1632 belonged to Sherley and the other London partners in the "Undertakers"; it was lost on its way to Virginia bearing 800 pounds of beaver as returns, Bradford, *op. cit.*, 254–255.

[35] Pearl, *London and the Outbreak*, 126n., 147, 148n., 255n., 265; Bradford, *Of Plymouth Plantation*, ed. Morison, 104, 106; *Cal. S. P., Dom., 1625–26*, 430; *Journal of Sir Simonds d'Ewes*, ed. Wallace Notestein (New Haven, 1923), 77.

[36] In his explanation of the division of the assets and value of a single share, Professor Andrews appears to have applied the terms of the 1627 division to the 1640 list of "purchasers," *Col. Per. Amer. Hist.*, i, 285–286.

Goodwin, *Pilgrim Republic*, 292–295, is substantially correct in listing the 156 individuals who shared in the 1627 division of land. The total assets in land prior to division cannot be ascertained. See Bradford, *Of Plymouth Plantation*, ed. Morison, 375, 376, Robinson's comments; 194, 196, organization of "Undertakers"; 382, 214, cost of bringing over company from Leyden; Bradford, "Letter Book," 58, 65, Sherley on other partners.

[37] Bradford, *Of Plymouth Plantation*, ed. Morison, 94; *idem*, *History*, ed. Ford, i, 268n. gives £400 as total value of the cargo seized; this included some clapboards. The literary result of Morton's ignominious departure, *The New English Canaan* (1637), satirizes the "saints" at Plymouth, *ibid.*, ii, 75–77. Nathaniel C. Hale, *Pelts and Palisades* (Richmond, Va., 1959) included a lively narrative of Plymouth's fur trade, showing little interest in its business end and letting by a few inaccuracies. Bradford, *Of Plymouth Plantation*, 119, 163, 176, 178; Bradford, "Letter Book," 36, on amounts collected; *ibid.*, 112, 183, on boats.

[38] See Percival Hall Lombard, *The Aptucxet Trading Post* (Bourne, Mass.: Bourne Historical Soc., 1943) for description of that post. A reconstruction has been erected on the site. On the visit of de Rasieres, Bradford, *Of Plymouth Plantation*, ed. Morison, 202, 203 and App. vi; Bradford, "Letter Book," 51–55; J. F. Jameson, ed., *Narratives of New Netherland, 1609–1664* (New York, 1909), 110, 112.

[39] Bradford, *Of Plymouth Plantation*, ed. Morison, 200, 215–216, 242, 262, 384–385; Goodwin, *Pilgrim Republic*, 337–340; see text of patent and map in Henry S. Burrage, *The Beginnings of Colonial Maine* (Portland, 1914), 186–187; money spent for patent, 3 *Mass. Hist. Soc. Colls.*, i, 199.

[40] "Isaac Allerton," *New Eng. Hist. Gen. Reg.*, xliv, 290–296; Bradford, *Of Plymouth Plantation*, ed. Morison, 202, 198; 3 *Mass. Hist. Soc. Colls.*, i, 200; see also Bradford, *History*, ed. Ford, ii, opp. 79; *Winthrop Papers*, ii, 262, 205, 317, 329, 334–335, and iii, 2, 4, 102; Bradford, "Letter Book," 69.

[41] Bradford, *Of Plymouth Plantation*, ed. Morison, 216–217; Bradford, "Letter Book," 71. Morison reads this "peddle," *op. cit.*, 385.

[42] Bradford, *Of Plymouth Plantation*, ed. Morison, 219–220, 386–387, 22, 228; *Winthrop's Journal*, ed. Hosmer, i, 65, 66. Morison's note, by its placement, is confusing in identifying Mr. Peirce's ship as the *White Angel*. He correctly states further in the note that Peirce was master of the *Lyon*, which arrived in Massachusetts in February 1631, *Winthrop's Journal*, i, 57.

[43] Bradford, *Of Plymouth Plantation*, ed. Morison, 229, 230, 237, 232, 238–244; Thomas Lechford, *Notebook, Archaeologia Americana*, vii (Cambridge, 1885), 189–190, Allerton's 1639 testimony on the *White Angel* and *Friendship*.

[44] Allerton appears often in *Winthrop's Journal*, and in *Winthrop Papers*, ii, iii; in Plymouth's tax list and as an official, *Records of Plymouth Colony*, eds. N. B. Shurtleff, *et al.* (Boston, 1855–61), 1, 9, 21, 52. Bradford, *Of Plymouth Plantation*, ed. Morison, 241n., 244, 245, 250–251, 392. "Plymouth Colony, Wills and Inventories" (typescript), 1620–39, 4, 5; 1641–49, 44, for debts to Allerton. Allerton gave permission for his brother-in-law's debts to be settled first with his other creditors, *Recs. Plymouth Col.*, i, 20. *Winthrop Papers*, iii, 437, July 1, 1637, Winslow's remarks. For an estimate less harsh than Bradford's see Andrews, *Col. Per. Amer. Hist.*, i, 288–289, 289n.

[45] Bradford said the beaver yielded 14*s*. to 20*s*. a pound. On one occasion, however, the arrival of "the plimouth merchants great parcel ... brought down the price," *Winthrop Papers*, iii, 150. See also Bradford, *Of Plymouth Plantation*, ed. Morison, 238, 243, 390, 250, Winslow's refusal to accept the debts of *White Angel*, and Sherley's reaction; 288–289, quantities of furs, 1631 to 1636; 392, 250, Sherley's remarks on Allerton; 255n., Peirce's ship; 287, plague and low prices; *Mass. Hist. Soc. Proc.*, xlv, 619–620, Sherley's doubts as to who sent the furs.

[46] This contradicts Sherley's letter to Bradford, Sept. 14, 1636, Bradford, *Of Plymouth Plantation*, ed. Morison, 287, 288. The bill of complaint in Chancery and Sherley's answer are in *Mass. Hist. Soc. Proc.*, xlv, 611–623. Minor errors of form in transcription called to my attention by Mrs. A. W. Millard, may be corrected by consulting photostats of the original, P.R.O., C. 2, A/44/43, deposited at Pilgrim Hall, Plymouth, Mass.

[47] Bradford, *Of Plymouth Plantation*, ed. Morison, 298, 301, 309, settlement with Andrews and Beauchamp; Andrews' arrangements, *Winthrop Papers*, iv, 129–131, 257, 437; v, 2–4; Andrews, *Col. Per. Amer. Hist.*, i, 370, 370n.; Bradford, *History*, ed. Ford, ii, 289n. Morison seems in error in saying the cattle were to go to the "poor of Plymouth." See *Recs. Mass. Bay*, ii, 39, 89.

[48] Bradford, *Of Plymouth Plantation*, ed. Morison, 298, 302, 308–313, 399–402, 415–417; Bradford, *History*, ed. Ford, ii, 332n., 294n., 158n., 336n., on Atwood, Collier, and Freeman; *Winthrop Papers*, v, 3, Andrews' comment. Atwood, owner of a servant and house in Plymouth, was a business correspondent of Sherley, *Recs. Plymouth Col.*, i, 12, 47, 48; "Plymouth Colony, Wills and Inventories," 1641–49, 39. Settlement with Beauchamp, *Recs. Plymouth Col.*, xii, 128, 129, 130.

[49] *Recs. Mass. Bay*, ii, 39; Bradford, *History*, ed. Ford, ii, 333n., paid for Andrews are £490 or £534 9s. See *Aspinwall Notarial Records, 1644–51* (Boston, 1903), 21, Allerton's acquittance. On former prosperity and drop in cattle prices, Bradford, *Of Plymouth Plantation*, ed. Morison, 252–253, 310; W. B. Weeden, *Economic and Social History of New England* (Boston, 1891), i, 165–166; *Winthrop's Journal*, ii, 17, 23, 25. *Recs. Plymouth Col.*, xii, 90, 127–132, agreements with Edmund Freeman, Beauchamp's attorney. Bradford, *Of Plymouth Plantation*, ed. Morison, 428ff., Bradford's surrender of patent. *Winthrop Papers*, iii, 167, on Plymouth's pre-eminence in fur trade; G. F. Willison, *Saints and Strangers* (New York, 1945) and Hale, *Pelts and Palisades*, describe the expansion and decline of the fur trade. See "Plymouth Colony, Wills and Inventories," 1650–59, 105, 110, Bradford's Kennebec stock; *Recs. Plymouth Col.*, i, iii, vii, later fur trade and Kennebec.

Bibliography

Primary Sources, Manuscript

Goldsmiths' Company, Goldsmiths' Hall, London. Apprentice Book, 1598–1645; Wardens' Accounts and Court Minutes, Vols. p-v, unlettered (w), 1611–45.

James, Sydney V. Three Visitors to Early Plymouth. Typescript prepared for Plimoth Plantation.

"Plymouth Colony, Wills and Inventories," 1620–39, 1640–49, 1650–59. Typescript, Pilgrim Hall, Plymouth, Mass.

Public Record Office, London. High Court of Admiralty, Instance and Prize Court (Libel Files), Bundle 82, No. 124. Stephens and Fell, Ship, *Little James*, and Treasurer and Planters of Plymouth in New England. Library of Congress Transcript.

Specific references to materials used in the Public Record Office and Guildhall Library, London, are included in the footnotes.

Primary Sources, Printed

Arber, Edward, ed. *Story of the Pilgrim Fathers.* London, 1897.

Aspinwall, William. *A Volume Relating to the Early History of Boston Containing the Aspinwall Notarial Records from 1644 to 1651.* Boston, 1903.

Baxter, James Phinney, ed. *Sir Ferdinando Gorges and his Province of Maine.* 2 vols. Boston: Prince Society, 1890.

Bradford, William. *History of Plymouth Plantation.* W. C. Ford, ed. 2 vols. Boston, 1912.

— — *"Governour Bradford's Letter Book."* 1 *Mass. Hist. Soc. Colls.*, iii (1794), 27–76.

— — *Of Plymouth Plantation.* Samuel E. Morison, ed. New York, 1952. "Letter of William Bradford and Isaac Allerton, 1623." *American Historical Review*, viii (1902–03), 294–301.

"Letters of John Bridge and Emanuel Altham." *Mass. Hist. Soc. Proc.*, xliv (1910–11), 178–189.

Burrage, Champlin, ed. *John Pory's Lost Description of Plymouth Colony in the Earliest Days of the Pilgrim Fathers.* Boston, 1918.

Calendar of State Papers, Colonial, East Indies, 1617–34.

Calendar of State Papers, Domestic, James I, 1619–25; Charles I, 1625–49.

Cushman, Robert. *A Sermon Preached at Plimmoth in New-England, December 9, 1621.* Boston, 1870. Facsimile reprint.

Dexter, Henry Martyn, ed. *Mourt's Relation or Journal of the Plantation of Plymouth.* Boston, 1865.

Firth, C. H., and Rait, R. S., eds. *Acts and Ordinances of the Interregnum, 1642–60.* 2 vols. London, 1911.

Harvey, W. J., ed. *List of Principal Inhabitants of London, 1640.* London, 1886.

Hosmer, James Kendall, ed. *Winthrop's Journal History of New England, 1630–49.* 2 vols. New York, 1908.

Jameson, J. F., ed. *Narratives of New Netherlands, 1609–64.* New York, 1909.

"Will of Robert Keayne." *Report of Record Commissioners of Boston.* x. Boston, 1886.

Kingsbury, Susan M., ed. *Records of the Virginia Company of London.* i. Washington, 1906.

Lechford, Thomas. *Notebook. Archaeologica Americana,* vii. Cambridge, 1885.

"London Partners in New Plymouth, 1641." *Mass. Hist. Soc. Proc.*, xlv (1911–12), 611–623.

Morton, Nathaniel. *New England's Memoriall.* Boston, 1903.

Morton, Thomas. *New English Canaan.* C. F. Adams, ed. Boston, 1883.

Notestein, Wallace, ed. *The Journal of Sir Simonds d'Ewes.* New Haven, 1923.

"John Peirce of London and the Merchant Adventurers." *New England Historic and Genealogical Register,* lxvii (1913), 147–153.

"Pickering v. Weston, 1623." *Mass. Hist. Soc. Proc.*, liv (1920–21), 165–178.

"Plymouth Accounts." 3 *Mass. Hist. Soc. Colls.*, i (1846), 199–201.

"Records of the Council for New England." Charles Deane, ed. *Proceedings of the American Antiquarian Society for 1867*, 51–131.

Sainsbury, E. B., ed. *Calendar of Court Minutes of East India Company, 1635–74*. 10 vols. Oxford, 1907–35.

Shurtleff, Nathaniel B., ed. *Records of the Governor and Company of Massachusetts Bay in New England*, ii, *1642–49*. Boston, 1853.

Shurtleff, N. B., *et al.*, eds. *Records of the Colony of New Plymouth in New England* (1620–92). 12 vols. Boston, 1855–61.

Smith, John. *Works*. Edward Arber, ed. 2 vols. Westminster, 1895.

Visitation of London, 1633–35. London: Harleian Society, 1880–83.

Willison, George F. *The Pilgrim Reader*. New York, 1953.

Winslow, Edward. *Hypocrisie Unmasked*. London, 1646.

Winthrop Papers, ii, iii, iv, v. Boston, 1931–47.

"Wreck of the *Little James*." *Mass. Hist. Soc. Proc.*, lxi (1927–28), 148–151.

Young, Alexander. *Chronicles of the Pilgrim Fathers*. 2d ed. Boston, 1844.

Secondary Sources

Adams, Charles Francis. *Three Episodes in Massachusetts History*. Boston, 1892.

"Isaac Allerton." *New England Historic and Genealogical Register*, viii, 265–270; xliv, 290–296.

Andrews, Charles M. *The Colonial Period of American History*, i. New Haven, 1934.

Bailyn, Bernard. "The *Apologia* of Robert Keayne." *William and Mary Quarterly*, 3d ser., vii, 568–587.

Banks, Charles E. "William Bradford and the Pilgrim Quarter in London." *Mass. Hist. Soc. Proc.*, lxi (1927–28), 55–68.

Beaven, A. B. *The Aldermen of London*, ii. London, 1908.

Buffinton, A. H. "New England and the Western Fur Trade." *Publications of the Colonial Society of Massachusetts*, xviii (1915–16), 160–192.

Burrage, Henry S. *The Beginnings of Colonial Maine.* Portland, 1914.

Calder, Isabel M. "A Seventeenth Century Attempt to Purify the Anglican Church." *American Historical Review*, liii, 760–775.

Dexter, Henry Martyn. *The England and Holland of the Pilgrims.* Boston, 1905.

Friis, Astrid. *Alderman Cockayne's Project and the Cloth Trade.* Copenhagen and London, 1927.

Goodwin, John A. *The Pilgrim Republic.* Boston, 1888.

Hale, Nathaniel C. *Pelts and Palisades.* Richmond, 1959.

Harben, Henry A. *A Dictionary of London.* London, 1918.

Hartley, E. N. *Ironworks on the Saugus.* Norman, Okla., 1957.

Kellaway, William. "The Collection for the Indians of New England, 1649–1660." *Bulletin of John Rylands Library*, xxxix (1957), 444–462.

— — *The New England Company*, 1649–1776. London, 1961.

Lombard, Percival Hall. *The Aptucxet Trading Post.* Bourne: Bourne Historical Society, 1943.

Morison, Samuel E. *The Story of the "Old Colony" of New Plymouth* (1620–92). New York, 1956.

Pearl, Valerie. *London and the Outbreak of the Puritan Revolution.* Oxford, 1961.

Plooij, D. *The Pilgrim Fathers from a Dutch Point of View.* New York, 1932.

Prideaux, Sir Walter S. *Memorials of the Goldsmiths' Company*, ii. London, 1896.

Rose-Troup, Frances. *John White.* New York, 1930.

— — *The Massachusetts Bay Company and its Predecessors.* New York, 1930.

Rowse, A. L. *The Elizabethans and America.* London, 1959.

Scott, William R. *The Constitution and Finance of English, Scottish, and Irish Joint-Stock Companies*, ii. London, 1910.

Shaw, William A. *History of the English Church during the Civil Wars and under the Commonwealth*, ii. London, 1900.

Slotkin, J. S. and Schmitt, Karl. "Studies of Wampum." *American Anthropologist* li (1949), 223–236.

Smith, Bradford. *Bradford of Plymouth.* Philadelphia, 1951.

Stearns, Raymond P. *The Strenuous Puritan: Hugh Peter, 1598–1660.* Urbana, Ill., 1954.

— — "The Weld-Peter Mission to England." *Pubs. Col. Soc. Mass.*, xxxii, 188–246.

Thornton, John W. *The Landing at Cape Anne.* Boston, 1854.

Usher, Roland G. "Isaac Allerton." *Dictionary of American Biography.* New York, 1928.

— — *The Pilgrims and their History.* New York, 1918.

Whitebrook, J. C. "Sir Thomas Andrewes, Lord Mayor and Regicide, and his Relatives." *Transactions Congregational Historical Soc.*, xiii (1938–39), 151–165.

W. E. P. [Winslow, Edward Pelham]. *Memorial of Edward Winslow.* Winnipeg, 1920.

Index of Personal Names

Cradock, Matthew
Cushman, Robert
Davenport, John
de Rasieres, Isaack
Downing, Emmanuel

Eliot, John
Endecott, [John]

Ferrar, John
Ferrar, Nicholas
Fletcher, Thomas
Fowler, John
Freeman, Alice
Freeman, Edmund

Goffe, Thomas
Gorges, Sir Ferdinando
Greene, William
Gudburn, Peter

Harcourt, Robert
Hatherley, Timothy
Heath, Thomas
Hibbins, William
Hobson, William
Holland, Robert
Howland, John
Hudson, Thomas
Humfrey, John

James I
Keane, Benjamin
Keane, George

Keane [Keayne], Robert
Knight, Eliza
Knight, John
Knowles, Myles

Ling, John
Lyford, John

Martin, Christopher
Mayhew, Thomas
Millsop, Thomas
Morton, George
Morton, Thomas
Mott, Thomas
Mullins, William

Newbald, Fria.

Oldham, John

Peirce, John
Peirce, Richard
Peirce, William
Penington, William
Penrin, William
Peter, Hugh
Pickering, Edward
Pindar, Sir Paul
Pocock, John
Pory, John
Poynton, Daniel
Prince, Thomas

Quarles, William